P9-CQW-617

NISHGA

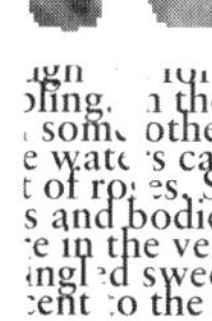
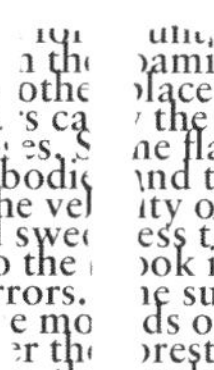
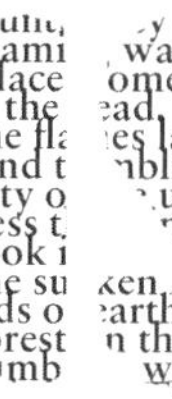
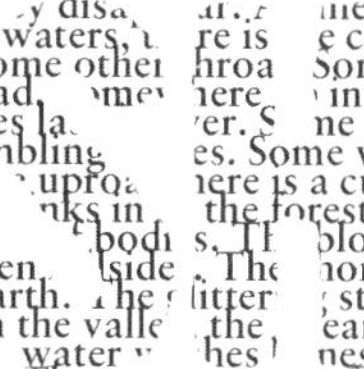

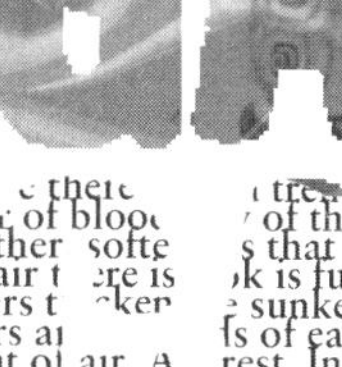

NISHGA

JORDAN ABEL

McCLELLAND & STEWART

For the Indigenous Peoples of the Americas

An Open Letter to All My Relations

It's taken me a long while to gather up the courage to
share this book with you.

This book has been difficult for me to write and for me to return to.

This is also a book with painful subject matter.

This book is about intergenerational trauma, Indigenous dispossession,
and the afterlife of Residential Schools.

It is also a book that is about sexual and physical violence,
lateral violence, depression, suicide, and self-harm.

While I ultimately hope that this will be a book that helps people,
I also want you to take care of yourself first.

If now is not the time, there will be another time.

"When the school is on the reserve the child lives with its parents, who are savages; he is surrounded by savages, and though he may learn to read and write, his habits and training and mode of thought are Indian. He is simply a savage who can read and write. It has been strongly pressed on myself, as the head of the Department, that Indian children should be withdrawn as much as possible from the parental influence, and the only way to do that would be to put them in central training industrial schools where they will acquire the habits and modes of thought of white men."

JOHN A. MACDONALD,

1883

"I want to get rid of the Indian problem. I do not think as a matter of fact, that the country ought to continuously protect a class of people who are able to stand alone. That is my whole point. Our objective is to continue until there is not a single Indian in Canada that has not been absorbed into the body politic and there is no Indian question, and no Indian Department, that is the whole objective of this Bill."

DUNCAN CAMPBELL SCOTT,
1920

"It is readily acknowledged that Indian children lose their natural resistance to illness by habituating so closely in the residential schools and that they die at a much higher rate than in their villages. But this does not justify a change in the policy of this Department which is geared towards a Final Solution of our Indian Problem."

DUNCAN CAMPBELL SCOTT,
1907

"It is quite within the mark to say that fifty per cent of the children who passed through these [Residential Schools] did not live to benefit from the education which they had received therein."

DUNCAN CAMPBELL SCOTT,
1913

"I'm sick to death of the lateral violence in our communities! I'm sick to death of the constant stream of hate and ugliness; the identity-bashing politics and the cruel ways in which we judge and ultimately throw one another away. We're all trying to find our way home as best we can. Some of us were fortunate to grow up with our languages and culture, some of us were not so fortunate. Some of us have had to crawl back to ourselves with both eyes shut. And most, if not all of us, have had and continue to carry our family traumas and the effects of a system not our own. The Government's policy has always been to destroy our communities, our families, our individual selves. We are all trying to find our way home as best we can. Yes, it is good to hold one another to account, to remember our responsibilities, and the protocols that govern us. But we also have a responsibility toward one another. We come from the circle, which by nature of its shape has room to expand without breaking. Room for many hands. Room for many voices. Room for many experiences. Room for many who, by no fault of their own, have grown up disconnected. I ask everyone to think about this the next time you're tearing someone down, the next time you're hauling them out to be humiliated and shamed. These are not our ways. These are not our teachings. These are the teachings of the church and Residential School. In nehîyawewin, in Cree, the Old People say, 'peyâhtihk,' which if translated accurately means to 'walk softly around something, to give something a great amount of thought before acting upon it. For everything—our words, our thoughts, and actions are maskîhkiy, medicine. Everything holds consequences.' We're all just trying to find our way home as best we can. No one has the right to say who can or who cannot come home. Home is the lodge we were all given at birth."

GREGORY SCOFIELD,

FACEBOOK POST, APRIL 14, 2018

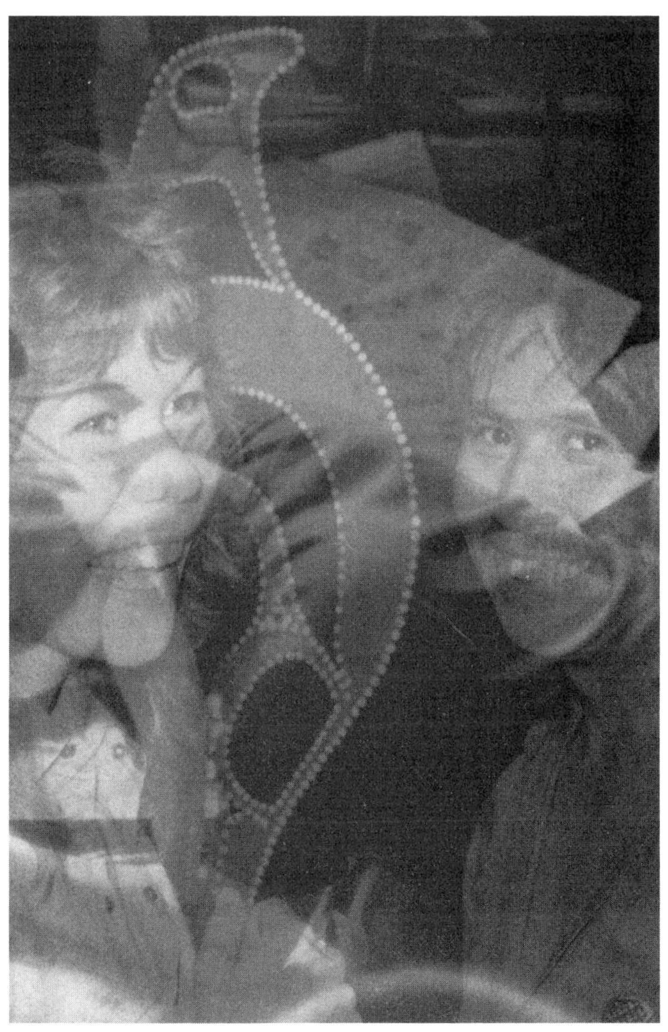

Scan of an oversized promotional business card

P.O. BOX 4554,
VANCOUVER, B.C.
CANADA, V6B 4A1

Scan of the reverse side of an oversized promotional business card

AN ORIGINAL DESIGN BY NISHGA ARTIST

Lawrence Wilson

Lawrence Wilson; Born March 22, 1954, in Prince Rupert, B.C., is of the Killer Whale (Giskaast) Clan of the matriarchal Nishga Indian Tribe. His parents are from the Nass River area, B.C.

In 1976, Lawrence was accepted by the Gitenmax School of Indian Art in K'san, in northern B.C. There he studied under the instruction of Vern Stephens, Ken Mowat, Earl Muldoe and Walter Harris. Courses in K'san were successfully completed in 1978. Two years later, Lawrence undertook an apprenticeship with Norman Tate, Nishga carver. In cooperation with other carvers he completed an eighteen foot and twenty-six foot dugout canoe. That same year Lawrence worked collectively on a sixty foot red cedar totem pole, "Big Beaver" in Vancouver. This pole was raised with ceremony in April, 1982 for the Field Museum of Natural History, Chicago. This event marked the opening of the Maritime Peoples of the Arctic and Northwest Coast Exhibit.

In support of his jewellery making Lawrence received a Grant from the Indian Arts and Crafts Society in 1982 and also in 1985. His work has been on exhibit in the Vancouver area over the years and in 1984 in California, Lawrence was featured as a prominent Nishga Artist at Pacific Western Traders in Folsom.

As a recognized Northwest Coast Artist today, Lawrence Wilson's accomplishments include a successful series of silkscreen prints, portrait masks, carved and painted panels and a variety of other items.

P.O. BOX 4554, VANCOUVER, B.C. CANADA V6B 4A1

"Too many Canadians know little or nothing about the deep historical roots of these conflicts. This lack of historical knowledge has serious consequences for First Nations, Inuit, and Métis Peoples, and for Canada as a whole."

Honouring the Truth, Reconciling for the Future: Summary of the Final Report of the Truth and Reconciliation Commission of Canada

Notes

I remember being at a club on Granville Street watching a band. I figured out later that I loved this band. But at the time it was just a band that I had heard of. I was there with a friend of a friend. She had come with me because I had asked her to. At some point my phone rang and I stepped outside onto the street. My Dad was on the line. We hadn't ever really had a conversation before. Actually, this was the first time we had ever spoken to each other. I had come to Vancouver that summer to see if I could find him, and after calling dozens of places, I finally managed to leave a message with a stranger who confirmed that my Dad lived there. I don't fully recall what we said to each other. It was all so unreal. Is that your voice? Is this what you sound like? What are we supposed to talk about when it's been twenty-three years of silence? What I do remember is that we worked out some plans to meet the following day. I was going to go to Waterfront Station at some specific time in the early afternoon and hope that I recognized this person I'd never met before. If I had been more organized I might have told him what I was going to be wearing or asked him what he looked like. When I finally went back inside the club I was in a daze. The band played a song and then another song and I started to feel okay again. When the music paused, the lead singer said, "It's Father's Day today. This is a song about my father. So that's a thing." The song turned out to be dark and dreamy, ambient and without words.

Interview with Jordan Abel by Sachiko Murakami for The Hardest Thing About Being a Writer, *published on January 12, 2017*

SACHIKO MURAKAMI: So, Jordan. What's the hardest thing about being a writer?

JORDAN ABEL: You know, I don't think I've ever articulated this before, or at least not in this way. But I think one of the hardest parts of being a writer is dealing with discrimination. For me, this manifests mostly as racism. But, that being said, I know numerous other writers who have experienced other forms of discrimination based on gender, sexuality, age, ability, and class. I think what's so difficult about dealing with, coping with, and resisting individual acts of discrimination is that we, as the targets of those discriminatory acts, actually have to deal with it. Really, we've got no choice. Whether we want to or not, we have to deal with it. It's exhausting.

So, for example, I went to the Denman Island Readers and Writers Festival this year. I was a bit unlucky because I got the first slot on the first day and almost the last slot on the last day. So I was, more or less, committed to being at the festival for the duration. Literally, the first question I got after finishing my first performance was about how much white blood I had in me. I think she actually said, "How much white blood do you have in you?" In response I said, "My blood is red," and moved to the next question. Later the next day, I was having a conversation with my friend who was also an author performing at the festival, and the same person came up to me again. This time, she told me that the last Indigenous writer to come to the festival had killed himself and that I shouldn't kill myself. Which was a totally fucked up thing to say. My friend was shocked by this interaction, and did his best to intervene. But, needless to say, it was a situation that I wanted to remove myself from as quickly as possible. If I didn't have another event that I needed to stick around to participate in, I would have just left. I mean, that's also the difficulty of that kind of festival in a remote-ish place. But I guess that's another issue.

SM: First of all—UGH. I am sorry that you were treated so badly. I send you many hugs.

This experience makes me think about how hard it is to be a racialized person in general—how (white) people's curiosity about difference leads them to make stupid, hurtful conversation. It's really no comparison to your experience, but as an example, I get grilled on my ethnicity whenever I give my name at Starbucks for a coffee order. Baristas stare at my face like I'm a dog at the dog park and they're trying to guess my breed. "My father was Japanese-Canadian," I finally say, and their faces light up. "I knew it!" they say, like they've just won a prize, and that prize is my degradation. Then they continue to grill me on whether or not I speak Japanese, and why not, and what a shame that is, and I'm just like, can I have my latte, please?

I'm wondering if one could come up with some sort of set statement to say before public appearances, to let (white) people know that people of colour aren't up for a race conversation. You say your friend was there and tried to intervene—I would like one of those friends with me, always. Maybe we can hire handlers who can field these conversations for us.

As a writer whose books bring Indigenous identity and issues into a usually mostly white reading and performance space, have you developed any strategies to deal with these unwanted conversations? Have organizers or moderators showed any kind of sensitivity to the issue of you being an Indigenous person walking into a mostly white room?

JA: Ah, I totally hear you! For some reason, some people—and here I want to say mostly white people but some racialized people too—project on us and/or expect us to perform their expectations of us. What's so strange about that, I think, is that we very often don't fit those expectations/projections. And, I would argue, that is because those expectations/projections are deeply flawed. I always feel this acutely when the subject of language comes up. So I'm glad you brought that up! I feel like I have often had similar experiences to the one you described.

Often people will ask me what it was like growing up in Nisga'a territory or ask me if I speak Nisga'a. I didn't. And I don't. Although

I really would love to learn at some point. Actually, at the Denman Island Readers and Writers Festival this year, my second event was a Q&A with a few other authors, and the host of the event interviewed each of us individually. And the first question he asked me was, "What was it like growing up in Nisga'a territory?" In all fairness to the interviewer, I was a somewhat last-minute addition to the festival because of a cancellation, so I don't believe he had as much time as he would have liked to prepare. But what really frustrated me about that question, and about that assumption, was that it carried with it this flawed belief that all Indigenous Peoples are born in their home communities. That all Indigenous people grew up speaking an Indigenous language. Or even just had a close connection, somehow, to family and friends that still live in that community. This assumption is totally flawed.

I grew up on the other side of the country from my community. I grew up with the settler side of my family in Ontario. I honestly did not even meet another Nisga'a person, with the exception of those that I met when I was an infant, until I was twenty-two. For me, personally, that has always stung a bit. I would have loved to have a closer connection to my community when I was growing up. Even now I would love to. But none of my family lives there anymore. In any case, when that question comes up—when they ask me about my experience growing up in my community or my ability to speak the Nisga'a language—it opens up a gaping hole in my heart.

All of this leads me to wonder why they ask us questions like that in the first place. And I think the reason is that they genuinely don't understand what it means to be Indigenous, to be an intergenerational survivor of Residential Schools, or to experience life as an Indigenous person in a primarily urban setting. Or, even more generally, they don't truly understand non-white, non-settler experiences.

Coming back to your question, though, I'm not sure if I have had that many moderators/organizers who have helped me deal with questions like this. For poetry readings, I've found most organizers are really hands-off once they introduce you. The way I've experienced it is that once you step up to the microphone, the whole floor is yours until you walk away. In an academic context, though,

I do find that moderators of panels and/or fellow panelists will often step in if things start to go sideways. I really think your solution is the most enjoyable one, though. To basically have a friend/unwanted-question-bodyguard by your side at all times to bat away unwanted topics or inquiries.

All that being said, though, I would say that my fellow writers are the people that always seem to come through in helping me navigate difficult situations.

SM: I'm glad you have found support in your fellow writers. I really hope our community catches on that adding an Indigenous name to the bill isn't enough in the work of reconciliation and decolonization. If it were up to you, what mechanisms would we need to put in place to decolonize a reading/performance space?

JA: You know, as much as I've complained here about frustrating and ignorant questions, I do honestly believe that education is the key to decolonization. I mean, I think it would be such a dream if everyone that walked into a reading/performance space was deeply considerate, intelligent and knowledgeable about race, gender, sexuality, age, class, and ability. And here I should say that I'm pretty sure that most people are. But there are obviously some that are not. I guess the question, at least for me, then becomes whether or not the reading/performance space is also an educational space. And further to that whether the role of the performer is also the role of the educator.

Honestly, I'm not totally sure how to feel about this. In my other non-poet life, I am an occasional educator. And in the classroom, I always tell my students they can ask me anything. And I'm pretty sure I've reassured them with the old cliché that there are no dumb questions. Do I cease to be an educator when I leave the classroom? I don't know. Maybe? I'd love to be a full-time educator with the type of students that want to ask me questions all the time. But the truth, like I mentioned above, is that I am an occasional educator. An educator in a precarious employment position. My employer, when I have one, is barely paying me to teach inside of the classroom, let alone outside of the classroom. So when I'm in a reading or performance space, my intention is primarily to be there as a writer. After all, they presumably invited me there as a writer, not an educator. And the work I do is also work that I'm interested in, and work that I hope others are interested in too. And yeah, I think it's possible to learn some stuff about Indigenous history from my work. But does that mean that I need to be or am supposed to be a general educator about Indigenous experience in Canada? Maybe? I don't know. I mean, I think that's not my first choice in that kind of environment. I would much rather be answering intelligent and thoughtful questions about my creative work. You know: the kind that some of my other writer friends get to answer. But if I am forced to answer a question or address a comment that requires intervening in some kind of troubling and, in my case, mostly racist discourse, then yeah, I definitely will do my best to make that intervention happen.

SM: A room full of people who have done the work to decolonize—from the organizers to the audience to the fellow writers on the bill—sounds like a dream. A dream I feel the urgency, as a non-Indigenous person, to work to make a reality, now more than ever.

If you could offer some words of advice to a new Indigenous writer who is about to walk up onto the stage in the mainly white room, what would it be?

JA: I feel like my advice would be this: you don't owe anyone an explanation about who you are, what you do, or how you do it. If you want to talk about it, that's cool. If you don't, that's cool too. I say this because I often feel like I get caught in this trap. Maybe because my work seems to invite questions like, "How can you possibly read this?" and/or, "Is this even poetry?" and/or, "What is this?" My reaction is often to try to answer these particular questions. And I think that might be a mistake. The people who read poetry, who are engaged with contemporary work, who are thoughtful . . . Those people never ask this type of question. They ask better questions. The people who ask me, "is this even poetry?" My feeling is that those people haven't read any poetry that's been published in the last 50 years. So yeah, I would say you don't owe anyone that type of explanation.

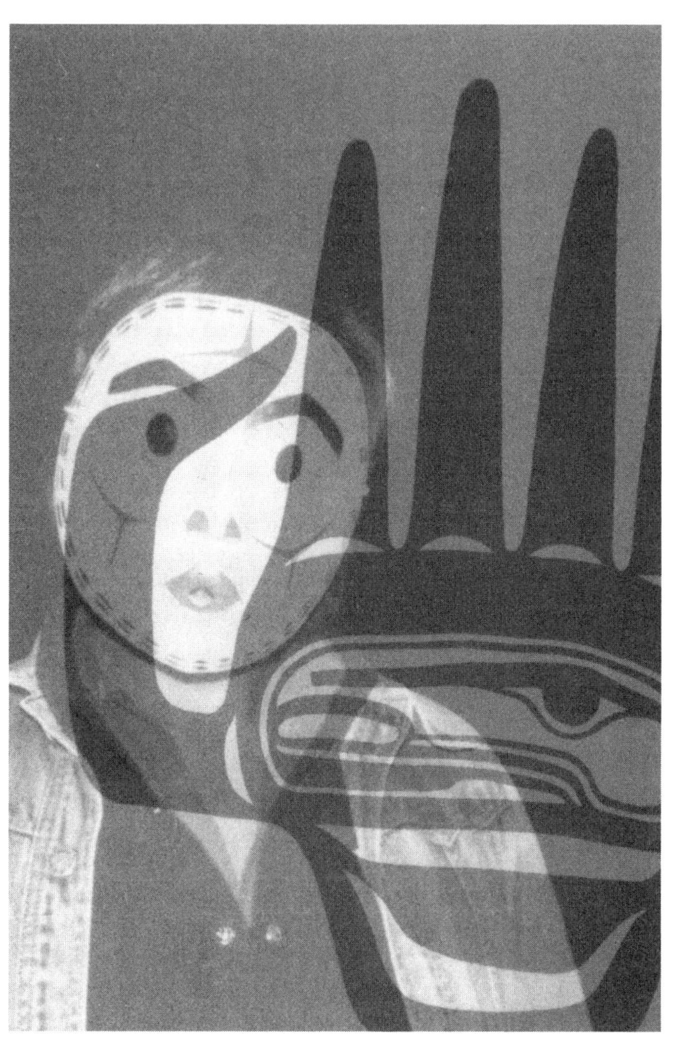

Notes

I remember sitting across a table from a poet I'd never met before. We were in a café somewhere in Prince George. I can't honestly remember the circumstances surrounding my visit to PG or why I ended up getting coffee with this poet. But I was there, and he was there, and we were both writers. So why not get some coffee together? My recollection of most of the conversation is hazy at best, but what I do remember with great clarity is the moment he said, "There aren't really any Nisga'a people. Not any real Nisga'a people. They don't exist." I can't honestly remember how I responded to that. I may have said absolutely nothing. But I remember thinking, "Of course there are real Nisga'a people. I'm sitting right in front of you." But I didn't say that. I just sat there wondering if maybe I wasn't Nisga'a enough to say anything. Maybe I didn't know what he meant. Maybe there was some kind of Nisga'a-ness that was unattainable. That I wasn't a part of. That I could never be a part of. So how could I possibly say anything if I wasn't a real Nisga'a person myself?

"Urban mixed-blood Native people in the large eastern cities must therefore wrestle with the logic of this apparently all-powerful dominant culture every day, where 'the Indian wars' have been declared won, where Nativeness is considered extinct and is recognized only as a fleeting, primordial essence, and where an Otherness that is mixed-blood or urban *cannot* be recognized. Urban mixed-bloods in these regions therefore routinely face demands that they 'perform Indianness' in order to have their Aboriginality recognized at all."

BONITA LAWRENCE,

"Real" Indians and Others: Mixed-Blood Urban Native Peoples and Indigenous Nationhood

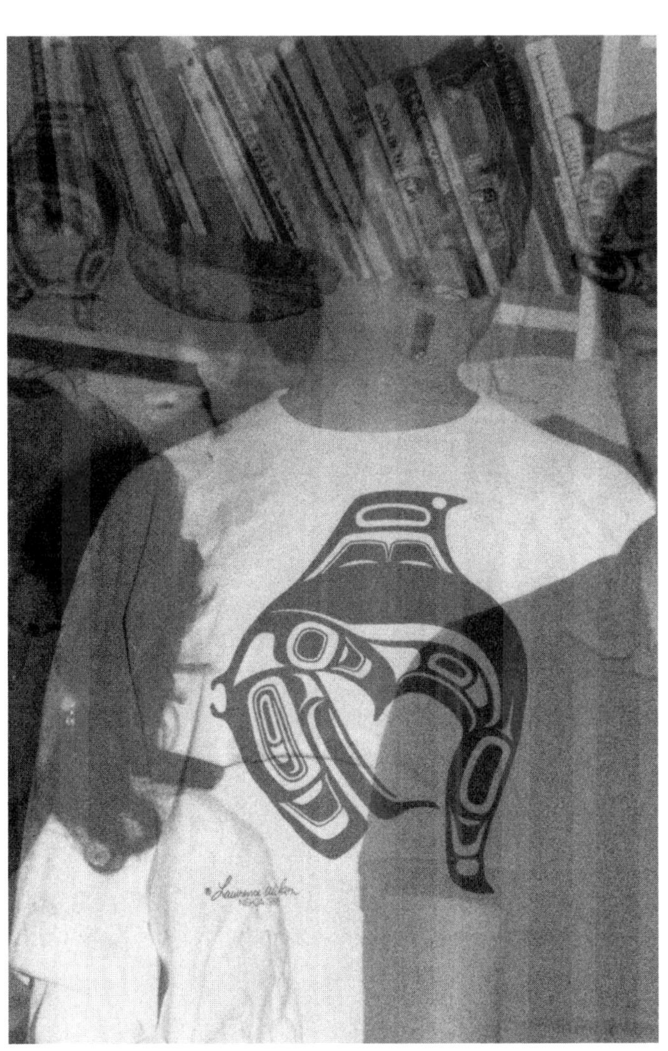

Notes

I remember being outside of a Broadway restaurant on a slushy night in Vancouver for a staff Christmas party. I wasn't really invited to the party, but my friend had insisted. So my friend and I were outside smoking, and some of his friends from work were there, and some of their friends too. We were talking and laughing. The food had been excellent and there was more than enough booze to go around. At some point, one of the friends of friends turned to me. She said, "Where are you from?" I told her that I was from the mountains. I had been living in the interior for a few months now, and since I no longer felt like a Vancouver resident, it made sense to me as an answer. "No, no," she said, "Where are you from?" I told her that I was from Vancouver. "No, I mean, you're Indigenous, right?" I told her yes. "So where are you from?" I can't remember if I had known what she was getting at, or if I was just waiting for her to clarify what she meant. But now I knew the answer she wanted to hear. "I'm Nisga'a," I said. "My grandparents were from Kincolith." I don't know how many times I've had to give that answer, but every time I do I can't help but feel like it's the only right answer, even though I'm not so sure that it is.

"How does one define identity? Is it the way we view ourselves or is it the way in which we are viewed by others? How can we reclaim our heritage when who we were or who we were supposed to be has been denied us during our most formative years?"

SHIRLEY GREEN,

"Looking Back, Looking Forward,"
Making Space for Indigenous Feminism, 2nd ed.

Notes

I remember talking with a colleague of a colleague at a book launch in Vancouver. She came up to me after my reading and wanted to talk. At some point, she asked me if I spoke Nisga'a. I said no and she asked why. But it wasn't just the question *why*. There was something else there too. She didn't say it, but she wanted to know how I could have been so irresponsible. How I could have been Nisga'a my whole life but never bothered to learn the language. As if I had access. As if I could just flip a switch and know. As if I hadn't wanted to. As if I hadn't felt that hole inside of me. As if filling it was that easy.

Logo of the Vancouver Aboriginal Child and Family Services Society

From the "Our Logo" *page of the Vancouver Aboriginal Child and Family Services Society website*

Laurence Wilson [sic], from the Nisga'a Nation, designed the Vancouver Aboriginal Child & Family Services Society logo in 1993. The translation for the logo is "Human and Wolf Child." As the wolf represents family, this is a perfect symbol for our Agency, which has been established to strengthen Aboriginal families. Laurence Wilson was born in 1954 in Nass River, an area located near the North Coast of British Columbia. Laurence apprenticed under Norman Tait for three years, a highly regarded West Coast artist. He also attended the prestigious Native art school, 'Ksan, in 1978. He prefers to use such mediums as wood, canvas, and hide in order to produce original paintings, drums, and two-dimensional carvings. With his extensive background in design and form informed by his culture, Laurence Wilson has become one of the many prominent Native artists in British Columbia.

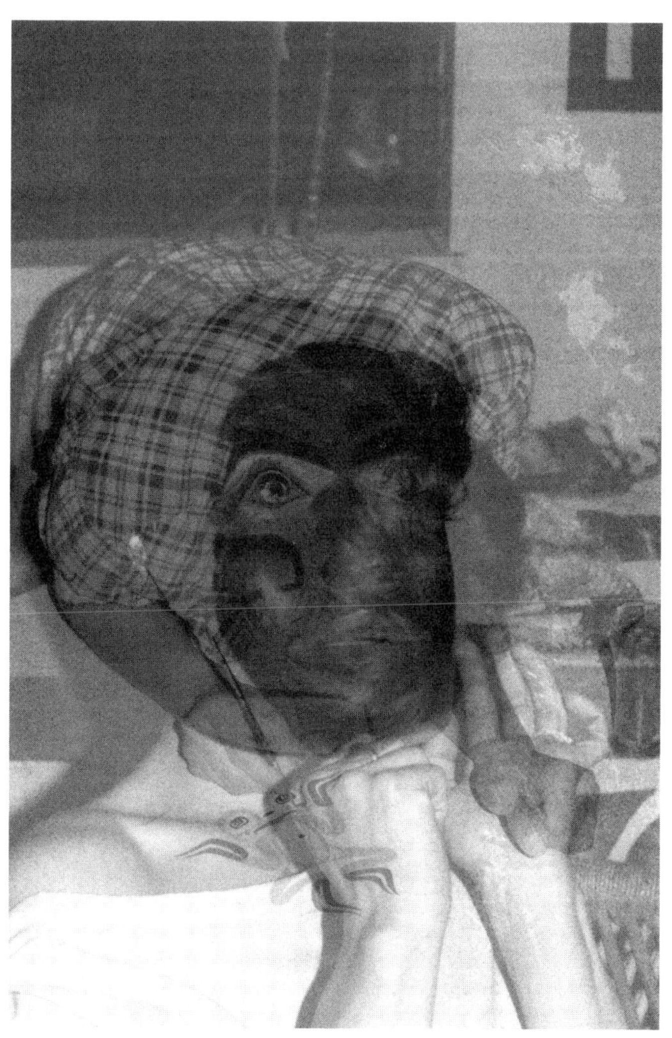

Notes

I remember being in the passenger seat as my mom drove past a small Christian elementary school that was just a couple of blocks from our new house. The public school that I was enrolled in was about seven or eight blocks away, but this school was right here. I can't remember exactly how I said it, but it was just a casual remark: "Why can't I go to this school?" I'm sure I said it because the Christian school was closer and in the winter I would have rather walked one block than eight. But somehow before I knew it, my mom had talked to some of her family, pulled together the tuition, and I was learning about God and singing hymns. At first, I didn't take it too seriously (even when they asked me to accept Jesus into my heart), but I just went along with it because I didn't know how to get out of it. Looking back on it, I don't understand how no one pointed out how strange it was for me to be there somewhat willingly. I don't understand why no one pulled me aside and said, "You know, kid, this is pretty fucked up considering all the things your grandparents went through and all the things Native people have gone through in general." But no one said that. I had no one to say that to me. When I walked out of that school three years later I was sure I was a Christian.

Excerpt from an audio recording of a presentation at the 2017 TransCanadas conference at the University of Toronto

15:19:35 Hey everyone. This might take me a moment. So please talk amongst yourselves. Stand up. Stretch. Do whatever you need to do. [Inaudible]

15:21:25 Hi everyone.

15:21:28 My name is Jordan Abel.

15:21:32 I am a Nisga'a writer from Vancouver, B.C.

15:21:39 I identify this way because for many Indigenous Peoples, these kinds of national identifications can indicate one's home, one's friends and family, and one's position within Indigeneity.

15:21:49 Likewise, these kinds of national identifications can often also be an indicator of which community (or communities) we are accountable to.

15:21:59 For example, Layli Long Soldier identifies as a "citizen of the Oglala Lakota Nation."

15:22:07 Louise Erdrich identifies as being of both Chippewa and German-American descent.

15:22:15 N. Scott Momaday identifies as being Kiowa.

15:22:19 Leslie Marmon Silko identifies as having Laguna Pueblo, Mexican, and Anglo-American heritage.

15:22:22 Marie Annharte Baker identifies as being Anishinaabe from the Little Saskatchewan First Nation in Manitoba.

15:22:29 That being said, these kinds of national identifications do not always adequately account for the complexity and plurality of Indigenous identity.

15:22:34 For some Indigenous people they simply do not tell the whole story.

15:22:39 For example, when I say that I am Nisga'a, you might assume that I grew up in Kincolith, B.C. like my grandparents.

15:22:43 You might assume when I say that I am Nisga'a that I speak Nisga'a.

15:22:47 You might assume that my writing reflects on Nisga'a knowledge, Nisga'a worldviews, and Nisga'a understandings.

15:22:54 Then again, you might not assume any of those things.

15:22:59

15:23:01 A few years ago during the City of Vancouver's Year of Reconciliation event, I was at a dinner meeting at a restaurant on Water Street.

15:23:06 I was one of a few poets that was commissioned to write a poem in response to the Truth and Reconciliation Commission.

15:23:10 The initiative was called Reconciliation through Poetry. The work that the poets were engaging with was meant to honour the work of Chief Robert Joseph.

15:23:15 At the dinner meeting, the poets along with a few administrators talked with Chief Robert Joseph, exchanged stories, and discussed what reconciliation meant for both Indigenous and non-Indigenous Peoples.

15:23:22 After a while, Chief Joseph directed his attention to me and asked me where I was from.

15:23:26 I told him that I was Nisga'a and that my grandparents were from Kincolith.

15:23:30 After a few moments, he said, "You're not really Nisga'a.

15:23:33 Some of my friends are Nisga'a.

15:23:36 Do you know how I can tell?

15:23:38 If you were really Nisga'a, you would have said *Niska*.

15:23:43 With a *k* sound.

15:23:45 Niska.

15:23:47 You said *Nishga*.

15:23:50 With a *sh* sound."

15:23:53 You know, I didn't really know how to respond to that.

15:23:55 My grandparents are Nisga'a.

15:23:59 My dad is Nisga'a.

15:24:03 But to a certain extent, he was right.

15:24:07 I wasn't born in Kincolith.

15:24:11 I was born in Vancouver, moved when I was very young, and essentially grew up in Ontario.

15:24:15 Does that make me less Nisga'a?

15:24:19 And what does it mean anyway to be Nisga'a? With a *k* sound?

15:24:24 And what does it mean to be NISHGA? With a *sh* sound?

15:24:32 What does it mean to be Nisga'a, but to have grown up removed from the Nisga'a community?

15:24:39 What does it mean to be Indigenous if your relationship to community has become severed somehow?

15:24:46 What does it mean to be both an intergenerational survivor of Residential Schools and an urban Indigenous person?

15:24:52 I think these are the questions that I've been struggling with my whole life.

15:24:54 I want to tell you about my life for the purposes of openness and accountability and transparency.

15:24:59 I think, especially now, when there have been so many thoughts and questions about how we define Indigeneity and who does or who does not count as Indigenous . . .

15:25:09 I'm telling you about my life because I am accountable not only to the Nisga'a community,

15:25:14 but I am also accountable to the communities of intergenerational survivors of Residential Schools

15:25:19 and the communities of urban Indigenous people.

15:25:26 I'm accountable to the communities of dispossessed Indigenous people

15:25:32 who are not able to find their way back to their communities because of an ongoing legacy of colonial violence.

15:25:37 I am accountable to myself

15:25:40 and I hope to talk openly about my subject position within the scope of Indigeneity.

15:25:43 Colonialism has had and continues to have a profound impact on Indigenous Peoples.

15:25:49 And some of that legacy of violence has been discussed at length; some of that legacy of violence remains silenced.

15:25:53 Here's a scene from my life.

15:25:56 I am twenty-two years old.

15:25:59 It's 2007.

15:26:03 I am an undergraduate at the University of Alberta in Edmonton.

15:26:06 I am studying English.

15:26:09 According to my official transcripts, I have taken art history, American literature, astronomy, sociology, spanish, children's literature, literary theory, and creative writing.

15:26:17 But to this point in my academic career, not one book by an Indigenous author has been assigned in any of my classes.

15:26:22 In fact, at this point in my life, I have never even met another Nisga'a person.

15:26:26 I mean, I've known some Ojibway people when I lived here in Ontario, and some Cree people when I lived in Alberta.

15:26:30 But the Nisga'a are from northern coastal B.C.

15:26:35 At least that's what I hear.

15:26:38 That's what I've read.

15:26:42 That's what I've been told.

15:26:46 But I've never been there.

15:26:49 I've never had the opportunity to get there.

15:26:53 So here I am.

15:26:56 A young Nisga'a person who has not only never met another Nisga'a person in his entire life, but is also painfully—

15:27:03 and I mean really hurtfully, deep down pain in your heart kind of hurting—

15:27:08 aware of the hole in his life where Nisga'a knowledge and understandings belong.

15:27:12 At that point, I think, the only book I had ever read by an Indigenous person was *Green Grass, Running Water* by Thomas King, and that was at least somewhat accidental.

15:27:20 I didn't read it because it was written by an Indigenous author.

15:27:24 I read it because someone had casually mentioned that it was good.

15:27:29 And it was good.

15:27:33 And sometime after I'd read that book I asked myself why I didn't know anything about the Nisga'a people.

15:27:39 Why didn't I know anything about myself?

15:27:44 Why is it that I grew up in Ontario but I was born in B.C.?

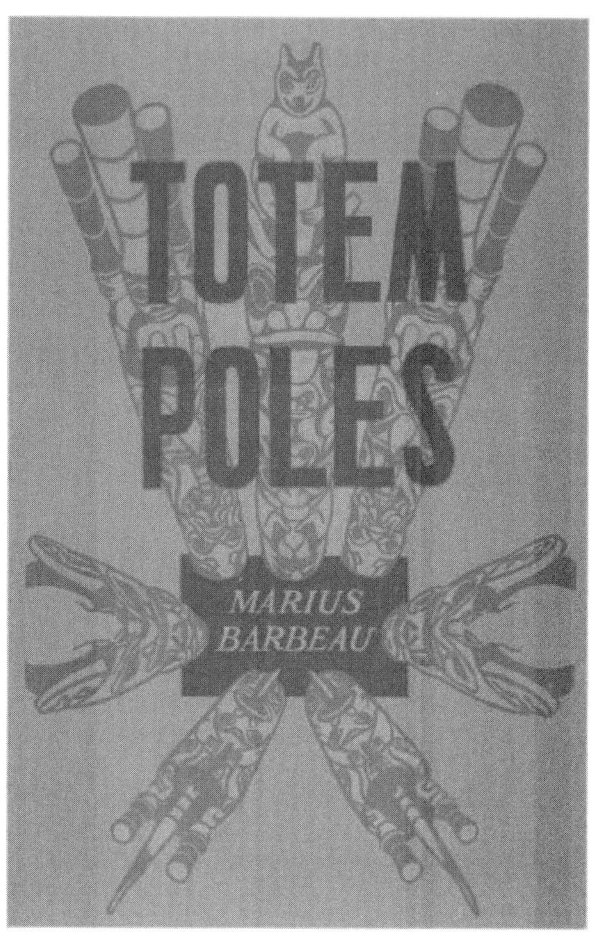

Slide 1: *Totem Poles*, cover

15:27:48 Why have I spent all my life not knowing the Indigenous side of my family?

15:27:53 So, being at least a somewhat dutiful student at the time, my first instinct was to go to the library.

15:27:59 So I went off to the library and I started to look for books using the search term *Nisga'a*.

15:28:04 The first book I found was *Totem Poles* by Marius Barbeau.

15:28:08 You know, I honestly don't know what I expected this book to be.

15:28:13 But when I opened it up there were stories about the Nisga'a people.

15:28:17 Which Barbeau spelled *Niskae*. N-I-S-K-A-E (Again, with the *k* sound.)

15:28:21 As opposed to *Nisga'a*, which is spelled N-I-S-G-A'-A.

15:28:25 But there were stories!

15:28:28 There was some hint of Nisga'a knowledge here!

15:28:33 I didn't articulate it in this way when I was going through this process, but what I was looking for was a doorway into Nisga'a knowledge and nationalism.

15:28:40 And without my knowing any Nisga'a people

15:28:44 or, I think importantly, understanding why I didn't know any Nisga'a people,

15:28:49 Barbeau's work was in fact a doorway—even if it was ultimately a deeply distorted colonial representation of Nisga'a knowledge and Nisga'a worldviews.

15:28:57 *Totem Poles* was an imperfect entry point and I had no other way in.

15:29:01 And Barbeau's book was filled with photographs of totem poles, and stories from the Indigenous Peoples of the Pacific Northwest.

15:29:07 But instead of providing me a pathway to Indigenous knowledge, Barbeau's work opened another doorway.

15:29:12 I began to wonder why I didn't know any of these stories.

15:29:17 Why didn't I know any of the Indigenous Peoples in my family?

15:29:23 In my book, *The Place of Scraps*, the main narrative revolves around the role Marius Barbeau played in dismantling Nisga'a culture,

15:29:29 along with many other nations in the Pacific Northwest,

15:29:34 by the buying and often stealing of totem poles and other cultural items from struggling communities

15:29:39 and very often struggling community members.

15:29:44 I make that distinction because in many cases he did make some kind of arrangement with an individual within the community, but it wasn't a community decision.

15:29:53 In the narrative of *The Place of Scraps*, it also becomes clear that Barbeau essentially stole a totem pole from the community that my grandparents were born in,

15:30:01 and there is a narrative thread in which I remember encountering this totem pole at the Royal Ontario Museum when I was a child without knowing or understanding its significance in my life.

15:30:10 It's actually just a few blocks away from here.

15:30:14 That, more or less, is the main narrative of *The Place of Scraps*.

15:30:19 But when people have talked about why precisely I use erasure in this book, I think most people end up missing a key detail.

15:30:25 Their suggestion that my erasing of Barbeau's words in some ways replicates Barbeau's own attempted erasure of Indigenous Peoples is, absolutely, part of it.

15:30:33 That by removing totem poles and taking advantage of struggling communities, Barbeau was actively contributing to colonial erasures.

15:30:37 Yes, I think this is true.

15:30:41 But the detail that is missing

15:30:45 —the reason why Barbeau's text is so important to this work—

15:30:51 is also because Barbeau's writing was the first imperfect glimpse I had into Nisga'a culture,

15:31:00 and that *The Place of Scraps*, in addition to being about Marius Barbeau and salvage anthropology, is also about what it means to be an intergenerational survivor of Residential Schools.

15:31:15 It's about what those experiences can look like,

15:31:21 and it's about having no choice but to learn about your own family history through the now-debunked work of a dead, white anthropologist.

15:31:30

15:31:35 Here, I think we've arrived at a good moment to pause for a second and to talk about Indigenous identity and position. Because it is helpful, I think, to frame urban Indigenous experiences and experiences of intergenerational trauma through these theoretical frameworks.

15:31:40 And to subsequently understand these lived experiences as not only being manifestations of Indigenous identity and position,

15:31:46 but also as being deeply misunderstood and under-theorized categories of Indigenous identity.

15:31:52 As Bonita Lawrence theorizes in her book, *"Real" Indians and Others*,

15:31:57 Indigenous identity is best thought of "as a negotiated and highly contested set of realities."

15:32:03 The way I've been thinking through Indigenous identity, then, is quite similar to Bonita Lawrence's thinking:

15:32:10 Indigenous identity can be thought of not so much as being fixed or static, but instead as being fluid, shifting, relational, "multifaceted and at times ambiguous."

15:32:16 In Deanna Reder's introduction to *Learn, Teach, Challenge: Approaching Indigenous Literatures*, she privileges the term "position" over the term "identity" as one that "undermines the object/subject dichotomy and makes visible the lines of relationship that affect one's perspective."

15:32:27 Reder's suggestion here to think through position rather than identity has been really useful for me,

15:32:35 and I think importantly shifts the conversations about identity away from the problematic discourses of authenticity.

"The central focus of this book is urban-mixed blood Native identity in Canadian contexts. It explores the tensions and complexities of Native identity when one is mixed-blood, urban, and either possessing or lacking legal 'Indian' status or band membership. Throughout this work, Native identity is explored as a negotiated and highly contested set of realities."

BONITA LAWRENCE,

"Real" Indians and Others: Mixed-Blood Urban Native Peoples and Indigenous Nationhood

Slide 2: Bonita Lawrence quote

15:32:43 My purpose in this talk is to address my positionhood as both an urban Indigenous person and an intergenerational survivor of Residential Schools.

15:32:52

15:33:00 Before I move on to the next slide, I just want to preface this section by saying that I am sharing these details with you not because I particularly like to share these things.

15:33:10 In fact, some of these details are still quite painful to share.

15:33:16 But I feel the need to share them with you in this context because I think it is important to understand what the experiences of an intergenerational survivor of Residential Schools can look like,

15:33:27 and where the difficulties are with communicating this type of lived experience to both Indigenous and non-Indigenous people

15:33:34 who may not have any idea of how these lived experiences are different from their own understandings of what Indigenous experiences look like,

15:33:43 or even what counts as Indigenous lived experience.

Slide 3: Dad, mask

15:33:50	This is my Dad.
15:33:55	His name is Lawrence Wilson.
15:34:01	I have met this man once in my life,
15:34:06	when I was twenty-three.
15:34:11	He was the first Nisga'a person I've ever met.

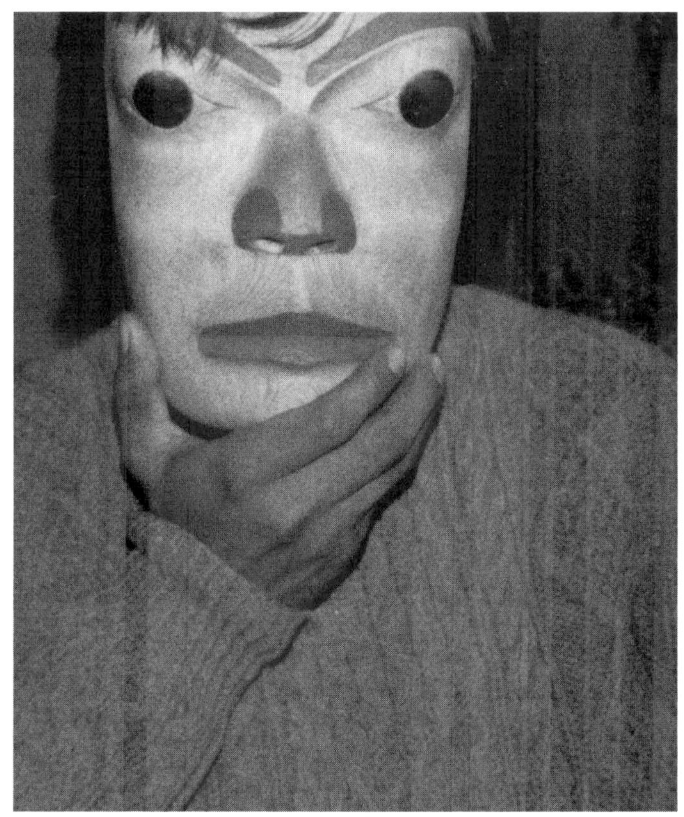

Slide 4: Dad, mask

15:34:17 He was a carver and a painter. He carved this mask. And this mask.

15:34:23 He lived in Vancouver for most of his life and mostly worked as an artist.

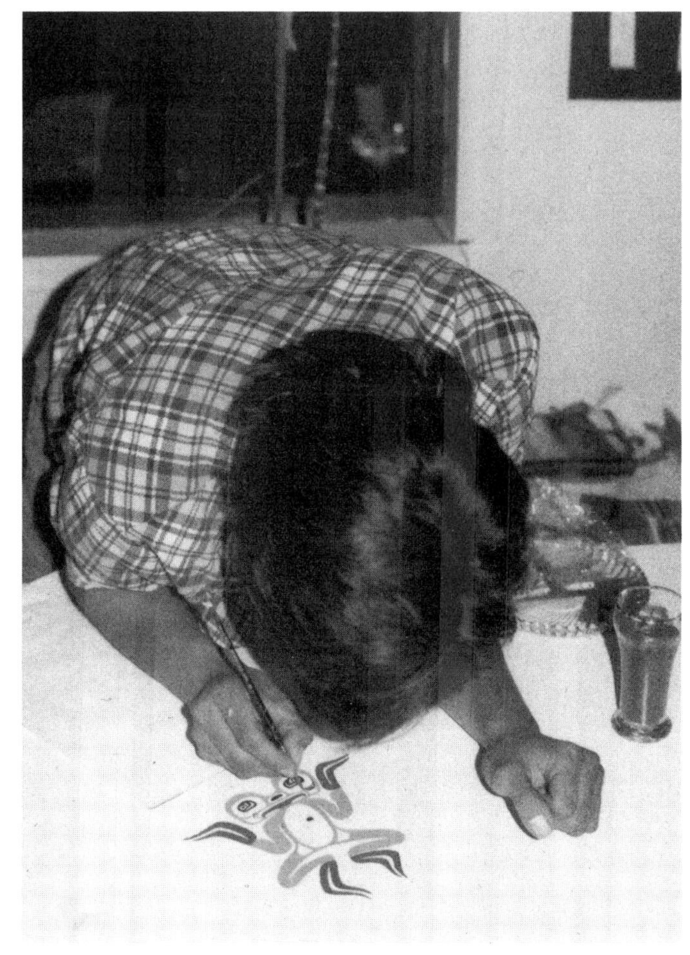

Slide 5: Dad, painting frog

15:34:27 Here is a photo of him painting a frog.

15:34:32 This painting is currently hanging on my wall in Robson, B.C.

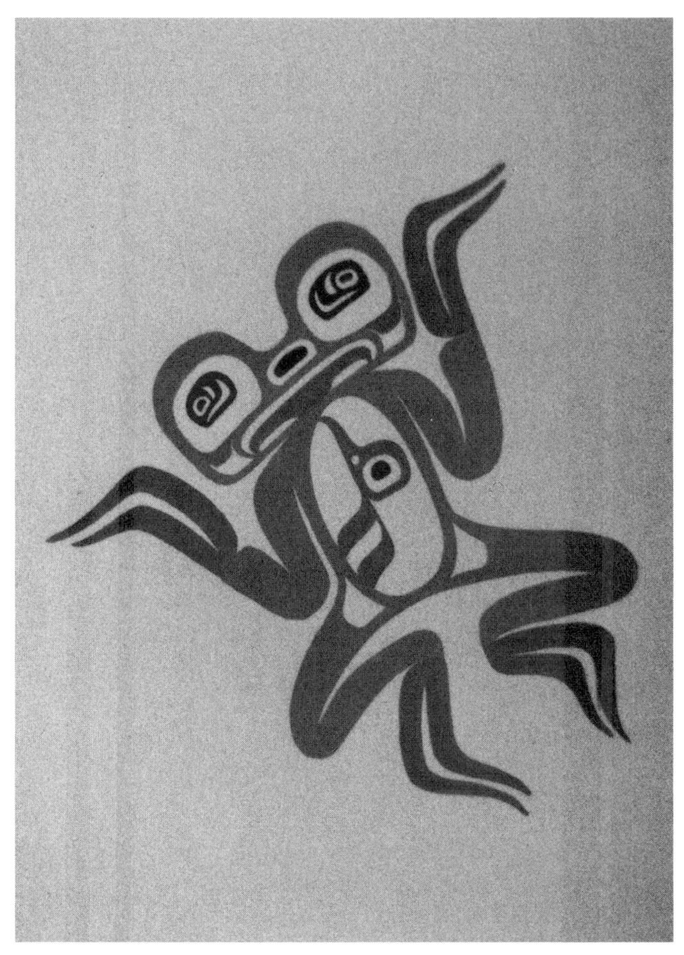

Slide 6: Frog

15:34:37 Here is the finished frog.

Slide 7: Mom and Dad, photo

15:34:41 Here is my Mom and my Dad.

15:34:46 Catherine Abel on the left.

15:34:50 Lawrence Wilson on the right.

15:34:53 They met sometime in the early 1980s, and I was born on April 13, 1985.

15:35:00 In an affidavit from the Provincial Court of British Columbia between my mother and my father dated May 8, 1996, the fourth line reads as follows:

15:35:10 "On June 15, 1987, Ms. Abel was advised by Det. Michael Miller of the Vancouver City Police Department that Mr. Wilson was under investigation for a possible sexual assault against a 15 year old girl."

15:35:19 Line five reads: "On June 16, 1987, Ms. Abel was advised that Mr. Wilson had, in fact, been charged with a sexual offence against a 15 year old girl.

15:35:30 Thereafter, nothing was heard from Mr. Wilson.

15:35:36 He neither exercised his access pursuant to the terms of the Order of May 21, 1987 nor contacted Ms. Abel in any way."

15:35:41 Line six reads: "In the Fall of 1987, Ms. Abel confirmed her instructions to us to continue to act as her agent as she no longer resided in the province of British Columbia.

15:35:49 Her instructions were that we should notify Ms. Abel of any inquiries from Mr. Wilson or attempts to contact her so that she could make appropriate arrangements for the exercise of the access to which Mr. Wilson was entitled by Court Order."

15:35:59 Line seven: "Ms. Abel provided our office with her forwarding address following her departure from the province of British Columbia."

15:36:07 Line eight: "We have received no inquiries from Mr. Wilson, or anyone acting on his behalf,

15:36:15 with respect to the matter of access to the child, JORDAN SKAI WILSON ABEL, born April 13, 1985, since the date of our appearance in court on her behalf on May 21, 1987."

15:36:24 Line nine: "At the time of Mr. Wilson's disappearance in June of 1987, to the best of my knowledge and belief, Mr. Wilson has been in receipt of income assistance benefits for a period of some years and was not in a position to provide support.

15:36:35 That fact, combined with his disappearance, resulted in our recommendation to Ms. Abel not to pursue Mr. Wilson for child support.

15:36:42 Given that she continues to have no knowledge of his whereabouts

15:36:48 or financial circumstances,

15:36:51 the likelihood of any family support from Mr. Wilson is too remote to justify the costs associated with pursuing such an action."

15:36:58 The affidavit summarizes my mother's departure from B.C.,

15:37:05 the sexual abuse committed by my father,

15:37:11 and his subsequent disappearance.

15:37:18 But what the affidavit leaves out is that Lawrence Wilson,

15:37:25 shortly after becoming a father,

15:37:30 was also emotionally and physically abusive.

15:37:34 In a letter that my mother wrote to me around 2008, she says that "when I was 7 or 8 months pregnant,

15:37:43 Lawrence revealed to me that his father had been violent to his mother,"

t15:37:50 that he had "broke her leg, knocked out teeth, etc."

15:37:55 Later, she writes that "not too long after you had come home from the hospital," that Lawrence's behavior changed.

15:38:02 She notes that Lawrence became pathologically jealous, and that he "began to take out his anger physically on objects—

15:38:10 threw a chair and broke it, crashed the baby's drying rack over the empty crib, and then clubbed me over the head while I was breastfeeding."

15:38:19 Later, she writes that she "finally got up the nerve to suggest that we weren't working out and should live separately.

15:38:28 Lawrence, apparently, took such great offence to this that he knocked me on the floor and smashed a large clay ashtray over my head.

15:38:38 He took off on his bicycle right after that."

15:38:45 Here, she notes that she departed immediately afterwards for Victoria where her brother lived and stayed there for two weeks to recover.

15:38:53

15:38:54

15:38:55

15:38:56

15:38:57

15:38:58

15:38:59

15:39:00

15:39:01 My first memories are of Ontario.

15:39:05 I lived with my mother.

15:39:11 None of the Indigenous side of my family was around.

15:39:15 She had told me that my father had disappeared

15:39:19 and that there was no way to contact him.

15:39:24 It turned out that this was mostly true.

15:39:30 I grew up not knowing and not understanding

15:39:35 why it was that I was completely disconnected from any Nisga'a people.

15:39:41 When I finally decided that I needed to figure it out,

15:39:46 I was eventually able to track down my father and several of my aunts and uncles.

15:39:52 But it was over the phone with my aunt Bonnie that everything in my life started to make sense:

15:39:57 why the Indigenous side of my family didn't talk to each other,

15:40:01 why I felt so isolated,

15:40:05 why everything was so broken.

15:40:10 She told me quite plainly that both my grandparents were survivors of Residential Schools.

15:40:16 In fact, they met each other in the same Residential School.

15:40:22 She told me that the best she could describe it was that her parents—

15:40:26	that my grandparents—
15:40:29	had learned how to be parents from Residential Schools;
15:40:33	that all of that sexual, physical, and emotional abuse they had been taught in Residential Schools essentially raised them.
15:40:39	And that when it was time for them to become parents themselves, they passed all of that abuse down to my father's generation.
15:40:46	I think, for the first time in my life, I understood why I didn't know any of the Nisga'a side of my family.
15:40:53	I understood why my experience of Indigeneity was primarily based around confusion, disconnection, and isolation.
15:41:01	I began to understand that, even though I never attended Residential Schools,
15:41:06	my life had actually been profoundly impacted by an intergenerational trajectory of violence,
15:41:12	and that the violence perpetrated by those schools doesn't just stop after the schools were closed
15:41:19	or after the apology was issued.
15:41:22	My position—

15:41:25 as an urban Indigenous person growing up in
the city without a connection to my home
community and as person impacted by
intergenerational trauma—

15:41:34 is one of disconnection and lack.

15:41:39 The reason why I ended up turning to
Barbeau's book for Indigenous knowledge can,

15:41:45 I think,

15:41:48 be traced directly back to the legacy of violence
created by Indian Residential Schools policy.

15:41:57 Here, I'd like to turn to a piece in *The Place of Scraps* called "The silhouette of a pole on the shore of Nass River."

15:42:03 The beginning page is, again, an excerpt from page 442 of *Totem Poles* by Marius Barbeau.

"The pole of 'Neesyoq and 'Neeskyinwæt, members of a Wolf clan at Gitlarhdamks, on upper Nass River. It stood seventh from the uppermost in the row of poles along the river front.

Description. It stood in front of a house called House-of-the-Sky (*wilplarhæ*) and belonged to the *ptsæn* type (hollow-back and carved all over). Its figures, from top to bottom, are: (1) mythical man with the deep sea cockle adhering to a rock (*kal'own*) holding his hand fast—illustrating a myth; (2) the head of the Sperm Whale (*hlpoon*), the jaw hanging down; (3) Person (*gyet*) wearing a garment with many faces on it, probably the Garment-of-Marten (*gwisha'dao'tk*); (4) the bird Gyaibelk, at the bottom of the pole. This mythical bird was also used as a head-dress (*amhallait*) and as a spirit (*narhnorh* or *narhnok*).

Function, carver, age. Erected in memory of a former 'Neesyoq by the present (in 1927) chief of the same name, an old man. It no longer exists. Carved by Paræt'Nærhl, assisted by his son, about eighty years ago.

(Informant, Dennis Wood of Gitlarhdamks.)"

MARIUS BARBEAU,

Totem Poles, vol. 2 (1950), 442

Slide 8: "The silhouette of a pole on the shore of Nass River," *The Place of Scraps*, page 47

15:42:11	The second page of this piece is then an erasure of the excerpt from page 442.
15:42:17	Here, you can see my focus on the parentheses in the original excerpt.

(*wilplarhæ*) (

) ( )

(*kal'own*)

( )

(*hlpoon*) ( ) (*gyet*)

(*gwisha'dao'tk*) ( )

(*amhallait*)

(*narhnorh* *narhnok*)

( )

( )

Slide 9: "The silhouette of a pole on the shore of Nass River," *The Place of Scraps*, page 49

15:42:23 Here, on the third page, there are just the parentheses.

(   )   (
)   ( )
                                 (   )
                      ( )
(   )   ( )   (   )

(   ) ( )
                                    (   )
      (   )

         (   )

   (   )

Slide 10: “The silhouette of a pole on the shore of Nass River,” *The Place of Scraps*, page 51

15:42:28 Here's the fourth page.

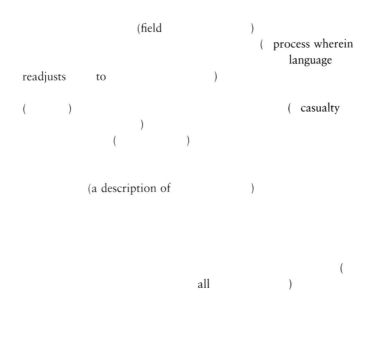

(field)
(process wherein
language
readjusts to)

( ) (casualty
)
( )

(a description of)

(
all)

Slide 11: "The silhouette of a pole on the shore of Nass River," *The Place of Scraps*, page 53

15:42:33 And the fifth,

15:42:39 final page of this piece, we ultimately arrive at another excerpt.

The silhouette of a pole on the shore of Nass River. When I was satisfied with the day (field notes completed) and when my ears were sufficiently exhausted by the translations (a process wherein an informant evaluates the qualities of a speech in one language and readjusts them to suit another language), I made my way back to the river. The branches from the trees overhead dipped onto the path (noteable), and the needles bristled against my palms (a casualty of the ethnological process).

My informant (Dennis Wood), caught up with me at the bank of the river. He was out of breath, offering up my notebook in his hands. "You forgot this," he said, handing the book back to me. This gesture (a description of a bodily action) took me a moment to comprehend, but once I gathered myself, I patted him on the back and said, "Thank you." This affirmation was not lost on him, as he began to speak at once about the crested column that stood against the river. He explained that the man on the top was telling a story, and I gathered that he was comparing me to this man (as I had been endeavouring to learn all of their stories). Although I knew that I must be nothing like this man, I was flattered all the same, and did not object as my informant continued to speak.

Slide 12: "The silhouette of a pole on the shore of Nass River," *The Place of Scraps*, page 55

15:42:44 The erasures in this piece flow forward and backward and intersect in the middle.

15:42:51 Stephen Collis has called this intersection point "a hinge page."

15:42:58 The page in question, shown again here, is the middle page with the parentheses.

15:43:02 Here, there is a moment in the piece where the erasures from the first excerpt meet up with the erasures from the last excerpt.

15:43:10 The erasures, in this case, work in both directions.

15:43:15 The concept of the hinge, here, is really useful I think, because it ties together

15:43:22 and in a certain way stabilizes

15:43:26 the points of intersection between Marius Barbeau's anthropological work in the first excerpt and my historic fiction masquerading as Barbeau's work in the final page.

15:43:34 The hinge page as it is constructed in this piece

15:43:40 appears a few times throughout *The Place of Scraps*

15:43:44 where it symmetrically balances two sides of a poem and the hinge appears precisely in the centre.

(   )   (
)   ( )
                                         (   )
                                ( )
(   )   ( )   (   )

(   ) ( )
                                            (   )
         (   )

            (   )

  (   )

77

Slide 10: "The silhouette of a pole on the shore of Nass River," *The Place of Scraps*, page 51

15:43:50 However, I would argue that there are also asymmetrical hinges in *The Place of Scraps*

15:43:56 and they are centred around the material excerpts from Marius Barbeau's work.

15:44:02 Here, again, is the first page from the poem.

15:44:06 What I would like to suggest is that this page is a kind of asymmetrical hinge that, on *one side* of this excerpt,

15:44:12 holds my experience and position as both an intergenerational survivor of trauma and lived experience as an urban Indigenous person,

15:44:19 *and on the other side* of the excerpt holds my dismantling of colonial authority and simultaneous articulation of an Indigenous voice.

15:44:27 Here, every moment in which a material excerpt comes up in *The Place of Scraps*,

15:44:32 the moments that precede that excerpt are also the moments in which I, as the author, am attempting to grapple with my own experiences as an intergenerational survivor.

15:44:41 The moments that precede these excerpts are the moments where I am forced to search for Indigenous knowledge through Marius Barbeau

15:44:50 because of the ways in which intergenerational trauma has impacted my ability to connect directly with members of my community.

“*The pole of ’Neesyoq and ’Neeskyinwæt,* members of a Wolf clan at Gitlarhdamks, on upper Nass River. It stood seventh from the uppermost in the row of poles along the river front.

Description. It stood in front of a house called House-of-the-Sky (*wilplarhæ*) and belonged to the *ptsæn* type (hollow-back and carved all over). Its figures, from top to bottom, are: (1) mythical man with the deep sea cockle adhering to a rock (*kal’own*) holding his hand fast—illustrating a myth; (2) the head of the Sperm Whale (*hlpoon*), the jaw hanging down; (3) Person (*gyet*) wearing a garment with many faces on it, probably the Garment-of-Marten (*gwisha’dao’tk*); (4) the bird Gyaibelk, at the bottom of the pole. This mythical bird was also used as a head-dress (*amhallait*) and as a spirit (*narhnorh* or *narhnok*).

Function, carver, age. Erected in memory of a former ’Neesyoq by the present (in 1927) chief of the same name, an old man. It no longer exists. Carved by Paræt’Nærhl, assisted by his son, about eighty years ago.

(Informant, Dennis Wood of Gitlarhdamks.)”

MARIUS BARBEAU,

Totem Poles, vol. 2 (1950), 442

Slide 8: “The silhouette of a pole on the shore of Nass River,” *The Place of Scraps*, page 47

15:44:57	What I'm trying to get at is that I think you can read these asymmetrical hinges
15:45:03	and the materiality of Barbeau's work
15:45:09	as attempts to represent both the lived experiences of intergenerational trauma and the experiences of urban Indigenous Peoples.
15:45:15	After all, what does it mean to be an intergenerational survivor of Residential Schools?
15:45:20	What does it mean to be an urban Indigenous person?
15:45:26	What does it mean to be Nisga'a?
15:45:32	What does it mean to be Indigenous?
15:45:37	What counts as lived Indigenous experience?
15:45:42	What doesn't?
15:45:46	What does it mean to be an Indigenous person without a connection to a home community?
15:45:51	What does it mean to attend to the communities of dispossessed Indigenous Peoples who don't have access to the knowledges and languages of their Nations?
15:46:00	And who is allowed to answer these questions?
15:46:04	Thank you.
15:46:09	[Inaudible]

"The legacy of the schools remains. One can see the impact of a system that disrupted families in the high number of Aboriginal children who have been removed from their families by child-welfare agencies. An educational system that degraded Aboriginal culture and subjected students to humiliating discipline must bear a portion of responsibility for the current gap between the educational success of Aboriginal and non-Aboriginal Canadians. The health of generations of Aboriginal children was undermined by inadequate diets, poor sanitation, overcrowded conditions, and a failure to address the tuberculosis crisis that was ravaging the country's Aboriginal community. There should be little wonder that Aboriginal health status remains far below that of the general population. The over-incarceration and over-victimization of Aboriginal people also have links to a system that subjected Aboriginal children to punitive discipline and exposed them to physical and sexual abuse."

Honouring the Truth, Reconciling for the Future:
Summary of the Final Report of the Truth and
Reconciliation Commission of Canada

Notes

I remember being seven or eight floors up in a building at the University of Saskatchewan, talking with a room full of people who were there to interview me for a job. From what I remember, there was only one window but the sun flooded the room anyway. At one point, one of the interviewers asked me if I could describe the importance of my work. I'd been asked this question at least a few times before, but it was getting harder and harder to answer. The Colten Boushie verdict had come out just a few days earlier and that was all I had been able to think about. "I don't know," I said. "The more I think about it, the more I wonder about what it is that I'm actually doing. I don't know that any of my work is all that important when we live in a country that clearly does not value Indigenous lives."

"Reconciliation means more than just the restoration of our relationship. Our women, our people, have unaddressed grief, intergenerational trauma, as the Residential Schools severed the most important bond, that bond between [I]ndigenous children and their mothers and their families. This system exposed our children to a cycle of violence that continues today, but we know that violence is a learned behaviour and therefore we also know that we can unlearn this behaviour. We can make a change."

DAWN LAVELL-HARVARD, PRESIDENT OF THE ONTARIO NATIVE WOMEN'S ASSOCIATION

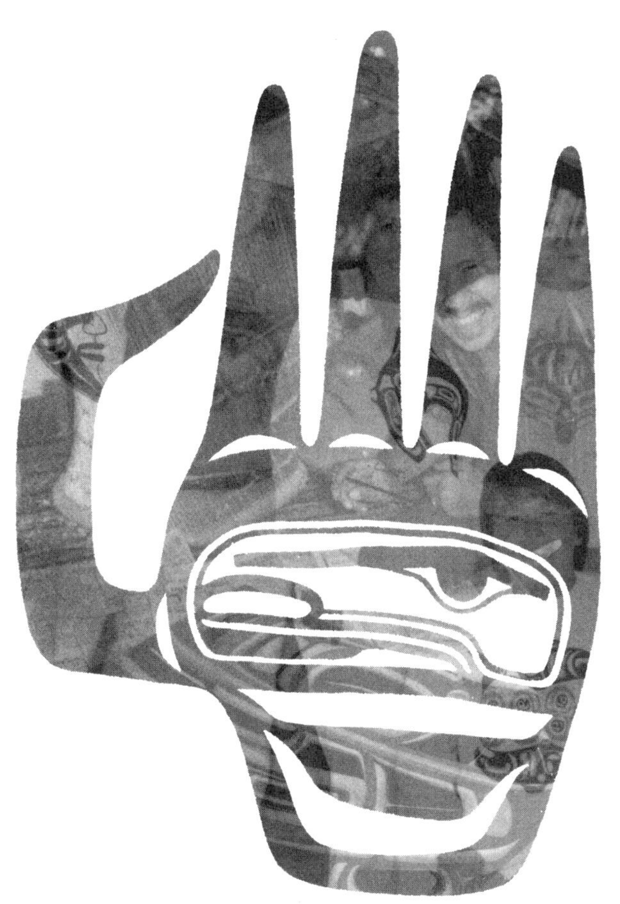

Notes

I remember talking to my friend as the news came out about the Tina Fontaine trial. "What the fuck," he said. "I just had to explain to all my bandmates last week why I was so bummed out about the Colten Boushie news. They don't understand. They don't get that feeling that we do. That Canada doesn't give a shit about our lives." We talked for a few more minutes and then he said he had to go out, go for a walk, clear his head.

"Over the course of the Commission's work, many Aboriginal people spoke to us about the children who never came home from Residential School. The question of what happened to their loved ones and where they were laid to rest has haunted families and communities. Throughout the history of Canada's Residential School system, there was no effort to record across the entire system the number of students who died while attending the schools each year. The National Residential School Student Death Register, established by the Truth and Reconciliation Commission of Canada, represents the first national effort to record the names of the students who died at school. The register is far from complete: there are, for example, many relevant documents that have yet to be received, collected, and reviewed."

Honouring the Truth, Reconciling for the Future: Summary of the Final Report of the Truth and Reconciliation Commission of Canada

Notes

I remember planning out some work trips with a co-worker. Every now and then, we would sit down together and he would say, "Okay, you're going to go out and cover Vancouver Island—do the Victoria, Nanaimo week—and I'm going to cover the high schools in Delta, Surrey, and Langley." This time, though, he said, "I think I'm going to take that Northwest week. Go up to Prince Rupert and Kincolith. It's a good trip. Maybe I'll bring my family. I'm sure you want to get back there. That's where you're from, right? That's where the Nisga'a people are? I'll say 'hi' for you."

Excerpt from one sheet of graph paper, handwritten in pink and blue pen by Catherine Abel

Vancouver Police Department— phone ~~438-4204~~
(604) 665-3535 non-emergency

-Detective Mike Miller
-Contacted C. Abel on June 11 1987
-L.W. charged with sexual assault to 15 yr. old girl
sec. 246 of Criminal Code—Sexual Assault

*C. Abel was living then at 473 Keefer St. Mau Dan Gardens Co-op

Victoria, BC:

Native Womens' Sexual Assault Centre 652-2788
Women's Transition House 385-6611

POLICE—Victoria City 995-7654

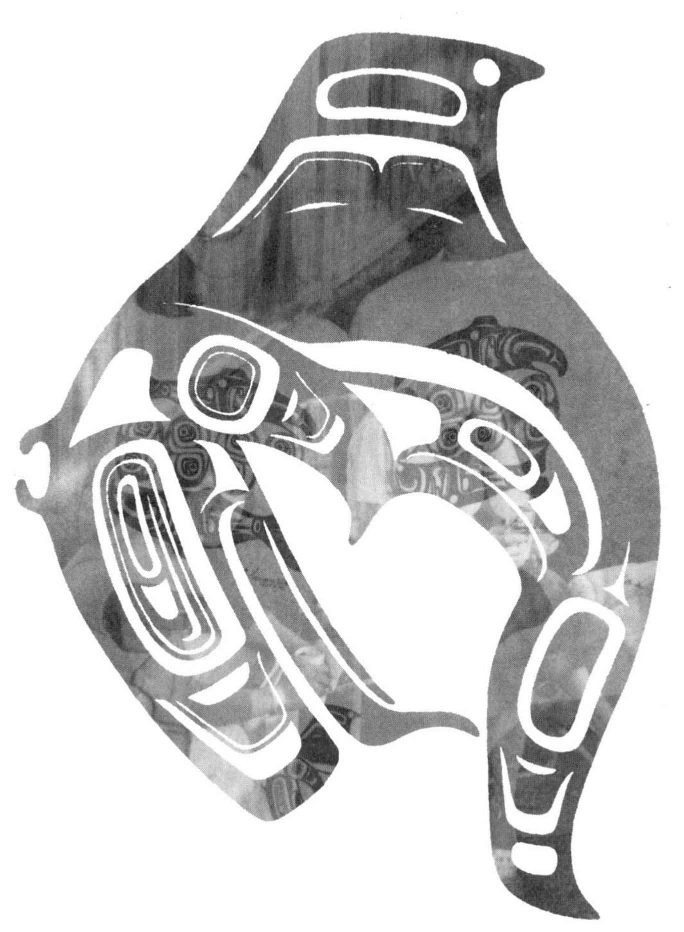

Excerpt from yellow Province of British Columbia pamphlet titled "Confidentiality and The Family Court Counsellor"

If you have decided to work with a Family Court Counsellor, it means that you want to settle some of the important issues that come up when a family separates. These issues concern your responsibilities to your children if you have children, and the future of your family. There are some things we would like you to know about working with a Family Court Counsellor. Although the Counsellor will explain them to you, it may be helpful to have this information in writing.

1. Your Counsellor is appointed by the Attorney General of B.C. and is trained and experienced in helping separating and divorced families. Although a Family Court Counsellor is not a lawyer and cannot give you legal advice, he or she has a good knowledge of court processes concerning family separation and divorce.
2. Family Court Counsellors do not take sides but help both spouses make decisions and reach agreements if possible.
3. If you have children, the Family Court Counsellor will help you ensure that these decisions are made with careful consideration of the children's best interests.
4. You have the right to consult a lawyer about any aspect of your separation and to have a lawyer act for you. If you cannot afford a lawyer, you may want to find out whether you are eligible for legal aid. The Family Court Counsellor can tell you about the various possibilities for obtaining legal advice in your community.

Confidentiality

The law and the policies of the B.C. Corrections Branch which employs Family Court Counsellors, say that a Counsellor cannot tell anyone, even in court, anything that you told him or her in confidence unless you consent to the Counsellors revealing that information. The only exceptions to this are:

(a) if the Counsellor feels that your children are in need of protection from child abuse or neglect, he or she must inform the Ministry of Human Resources like any other person with such information; and

(b) if the information you give the Family Court Counsellor concerns a criminal offence or other federal law matters, the Family Court Counsellor is not required to keep it confidential, and may be required to give evidence.

Because the Family Court Counsellor works with both spouses and because communication is necessary to reaching fair decisions, you should advise the Counsellor if there is something you want withheld from your spouse.

Report

If a court orders a Family Court Counsellor to make a report, usually when the parents are arguing in court about custody of children or accesss to them, the parents have the legal right to have a Counsellor prepare the report who has had *no* previous contact with the family. However, parents can consent to the report being prepared by a Counsellor who knows them.

If you require more information, please contact your nearest Probation and Family Court Services Office.

"The high deaths rates in the schools were, in part, a reflection of the high death rates among the Aboriginal community in general. Indian Affairs officials often tried to portray these rates as simply the price that Aboriginal people had to pay as part of the process of becoming civilized. In reality, these rates were the price they paid for being colonized. Aboriginal livelihoods were based on access to the land; colonization disrupted that access and introduced new illnesses to North America. Colonial policies helped wipe out food sources and confined Aboriginal people to poorly located reserves, with inadequate sanitation and shelter."

Honouring the Truth, Reconciling for the Future: Summary of the Final Report of the Truth and Reconciliation Commission of Canada

Notes

I remember turning the spoon over and over in my hands. This is a spoon that my father carved. He held it, and now I'm holding it. I'm seeing it for the first time, feeling its lightness. In a room with two strangers who knew my father years ago. Who knew my father before his disappearance, before the sexual assault. They didn't know him after, though. Those connections had been broken a long time ago. But they seemed to remember him fondly.

"As the numbers demonstrate, the abuse of children was rampant. From 1958, when it first opened, until 1979, there was never a year in which Grollier Hall in Inuvik did not employ at least one dormitory supervisor who would later be convicted for sexually abusing students at the school."

Honouring the Truth, Reconciling for the Future: Summary of the Final Report of the Truth and Reconciliation Commission of Canada

Notes

I remember being asked, *so, where are you from?* or *where are you really from?* or *don't all you Indians get free university?* or *where are you from?* or *why don't you go back to your reserve?* or *why don't you speak your language?* or *so what are you?* or *where are you from?* or *aren't you people good with cell phones?* or *are you adopted?* or *shouldn't you be out in a teepee somewhere?* or *where are you from?* or *don't you think you're being too hard on the Washington Redskins?* or *can't we just stop being political for just one minute?* or *where are you from?* or *don't all lives matter, though?* or *why don't you go back to China?* or *where are you from?*

Excerpt from a scrap of lined paper handwritten in blue ink, found behind a photograph of silkscreened graphic T-shirts

PRICE BREAKS

100%	0–24	=	$10.00	
	25–48	=	9.50	
	49–84	=	9.00	
	84–168	=	8.00	
	over 168	=	7.00	(our cost!)
50/50	0–24	=	$8.00	
	25–48	=	7.50	
	49–84	=	7.00	
	over 85	=	6.00	(our cost!)

"A recurrent theme in the family histories of urban mixed-bloods is loss of relationship to their communities of origin. Government policies of deliberate interference in Native family life, such as Residential School, loss of Indian status, and the forced adoption of Native children, as well as termination and relocation policies (in the United States) have resulted in individuals being permanently exiled from what was once home. The implications of this rupturing of ties to community, for peoples whose identities are rooted in a connection to land and other people, are profound. One individual referred to her family's experiences of loss of community as resulting in 'generations of loneliness, isolation, and alienation.'"

BONITA LAWRENCE,

"Real" Indians and Others: Mixed-Blood Urban Native Peoples and Indigenous Nationhood

Notes

I remember being at a booth at Hobiyee (the Nisga'a New Year) when I was working for a small Indigenous college in B.C. Somehow I managed to set up my booth right next to the folks from Vancouver Aboriginal Child and Family Services Society (VACFSS) and we started to talk. For some reason, I had forgotten all about their logo until I looked down at the swag on their table. There were dozens of gold-wrapped chocolate medallions that all had my Dad's logo on them: the "Human and Wolf Child." I stared down at them for what felt like minutes, but must have probably just been seconds. "My Dad painted your logo," I said. "He was a total piece of shit and a terrible parent." I don't know if that's exactly how I felt. But that's what I said. After a moment, one of the VACFSS people shrugged off the irony and said something like, "Not everybody can be a good parent." I asked them if I could take a few of their chocolates and they seemed to be fine with it. A few days later I was in my car, and had forgotten about the chocolates until I opened the glove box. I held the two chocolates in my hand for a few minutes, thinking that I should save them. That they were important somehow. But I didn't want to look at them anymore. I didn't want to save them. Everything about them was awful and wonderful and broken. I unwrapped one and bit in. The chocolate was partly melted from the heat from my hands, and the taste was overly sweet and artificial.

"Privileging a connection to ancestral homelands as a marker of Indigenous identity reinforces dominant visions of Indigenous Peoples as authentic only if they live in remote areas and engage in 'traditional' lifestyles or, conversely, only if we assume that these homelands are located exclusively in such areas. When the source of Indigenous identities and the focus of lifeways is located outside the urban milieu, innovations that emerge from interactions with non-Indigenous society are positioned as less central or even as less 'authentic' than transplanted tribal traditions. Different Indigenous relationships to ancestral lands are homogenized, and people who may not possess these connections are excluded. In particular, an emphasis on a connection to land and ancestral territories (as dominantly conflated with rural or remote areas) generates questions about the identities of urban Indigenous dwellers whose connection to tribal homelands may be sporadic, may not continue to exist, or may never have existed. It poses particular barriers for individuals with Indigenous and non-Indigenous ancestry who may not have had a strong connection to traditional, rural Indigenous communities (e.g., Lawrence 2004; Proulx 2006), and for many third- and fourth-generation urban residents (e.g., Jackson 2001)."

EVELYN PETERS AND CHRIS ANDERSEN,

"Introduction," *Indigenous in the City: Contemporary Identities and Cultural Innovation*

Notes

I remember being at a conference in southern Ontario right after my second book came out. I had just given a talk an hour or two before, and was still having conversations between panels about my work. At one point, an established and popular Indigenous artist came up to me and asked me point blank what gave me the right to work with and deconstruct the work of others. I think I told her that the work I do attempts to mirror the appropriative mechanisms of colonialism. But she was unhappy with that answer and unhappy with my work. Looking back at that moment, I am unsatisfied too. If I could return to that moment now, I would have said that I work with found text because that was my first real connection to Indigeneity, and, as an intergenerational survivor of Residential Schools, I create art that attempts to reflect my life experience, including my severance from Indigenous knowledge and land.

Excerpt from an affidavit written by Barrister and Solicitor Marnie Dunnaway

BETWEEN:

CATHERINE ANN ABEL

Applicant

AND:

LAWRENCE MELVIN WILSON

Respondent

Excerpt from an affidavit written by Barrister and Solicitor Marnie Dunnaway

1. I am the Solicitor for the Applicant, Catherine Ann Abel, in the matter of her custody, access and maintenance application in relation to the child, JORDAN SKAI WILSON ABEL, born April 13, 1985, and as such have personal knowledge of the matters and facts deposed to herein except where the same are stated to be on information and belief and where so stated, I verily believe the facts to be true.

Excerpt from an affidavit written by Barrister and Solicitor Marnie Dunnaway

2. I acted on behalf of Ms. Abel in this matter in the provincial Court of British Columbia at Vancouver in proceedings in May of 1987. Attached hereto as Exhibit "A" is a copy of an Order dated May 12, 1987. Attached hereto as Exhibit "B" is a copy of an Order dated May 21, 1987 in those proceedings.

Excerpt from an affidavit written by Barrister and Solicitor Marnie Dunnaway

3. Following those proceedings, I was instructed to continue to act on behalf of Ms. Abel with respect to matters of access as well as child support.

Excerpt from an affidavit written by Barrister and Solicitor Marnie Dunnaway

4. On June 15, 1987, Ms. Abel was advised by Det. Michael Miller of the Vancouver City Police Department that Mr. Wilson was under investigation for a possible sexual assault against a 15 year old girl.

Excerpt from an affidavit written by Barrister and Solicitor Marnie Dunnaway

5. On June 16, 1987, Ms. Abel was advised that Mr. Wilson had, in fact, been charged with a sexual offence against a 15 year old girl. Thereafter, nothing was heard from Mr. Wilson. He neither exercised his access pursuant to the terms of the Order of May 21, 1987 nor contacted Ms. Abel in any way.

Excerpt from an affidavit written by Barrister and Solicitor Marnie Dunnaway

6. In the fall of 1987, Ms. Abel confirmed her instructions to us to continue to act as her agent as she no longer resided in the Province of British Columbia. Her instructions were that we should notify Ms. Abel of any inquiries from Mr. Wilson or attempts to contact her, so that she could make appropriate arrangements for the exercise of the access to which Mr. Wilson was entitled by Court Order.

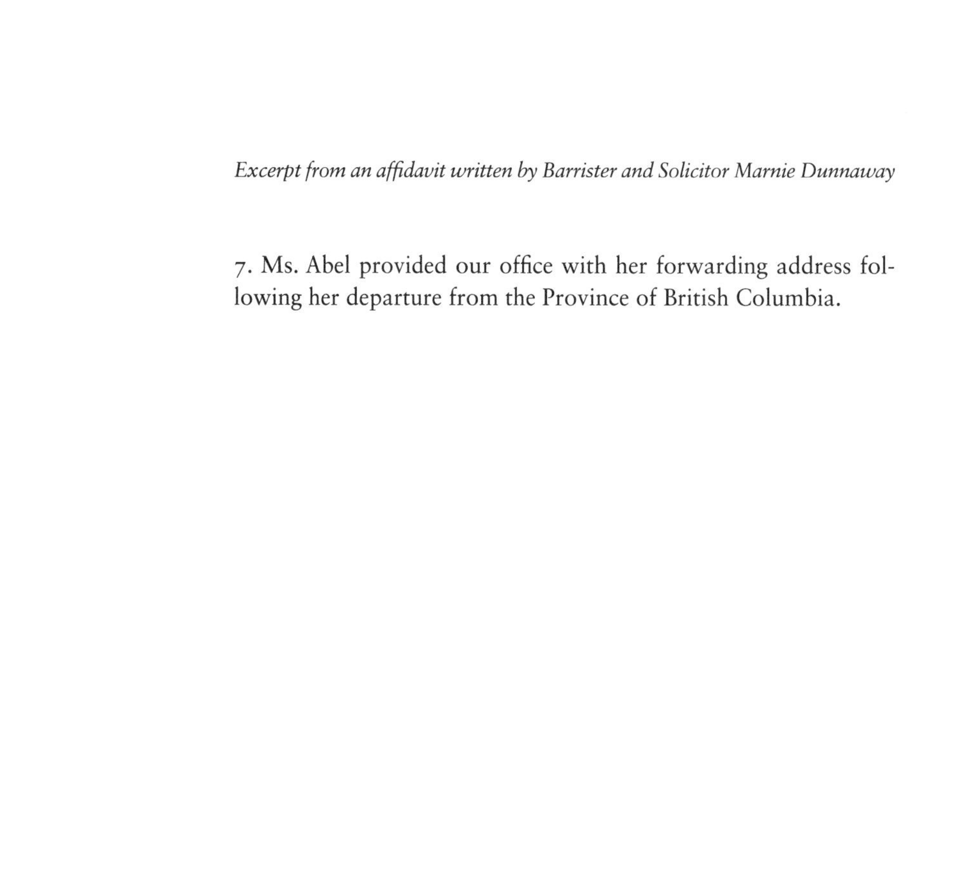

Excerpt from an affidavit written by Barrister and Solicitor Marnie Dunnaway

7. Ms. Abel provided our office with her forwarding address following her departure from the Province of British Columbia.

Excerpt from an affidavit written by Barrister and Solicitor Marnie Dunnaway

8. We have received no inquiries from Mr. Wilson, or anyone acting on his behalf, with respect to the matter of access to the child, JORDAN SKAI WILSON ABEL, born April 13, 1985, since the date of our appearance in Court on her behalf on May 21, 1987.

Excerpt from an affidavit written by Barrister and Solicitor Marnie Dunnaway

9. At the time of Mr. Wilson's disappearance in June of 1987, to the best of my knowledge and belief, Mr. Wilson had been in receipt of income assistance benefits for a period of some years and was not in a position to provide support. That fact, combined with his disappearance, resulted in our recommendation to Ms. Abel not to pursue Mr. Wilson for child support. Given that she continues to have no knowledge of his whereabouts or financial circumstances, the likelihood of any family support from Mr. Wilson is too remote to justify the costs associated with pursuing such an action.

Notes

I remember being in my mentor's office during my MFA. I had just written the first forty or so pages of my first book, and I was looking for guidance, for a foothold, for something to reassure me that the project of articulating my relationship to Indigeneity through Marius Barbeau wasn't a total waste of time. As she flipped through page after page, she made a few line edits here and there. Change this word. Cut this line. Think about this line break. Except none of that really made any sense for these erasure poems that were built out of old anthropological writings. At one point, she turned to me and said, "These are fine, Jordan. But when are you going to start writing some real poems?"

"As we stand in the presence of our Residential School survivors we are reminded of a system meant to kill the Indian in the child. Not only have they suffered unspeakable abuse, their children and grandchildren have also suffered. How terribly sad that this horrible legacy continues to impact our present generations, as so evident in the current suicide crisis of our children and youth. The vast majority of us as First Nations people across this land can speak of the direct impacts of this dark legacy. Yes, many of us have lived in the direct darkness and shadows of the evil that was so evident in so many of those schools."

ONTARIO REGIONAL CHIEF ISADORE DAY

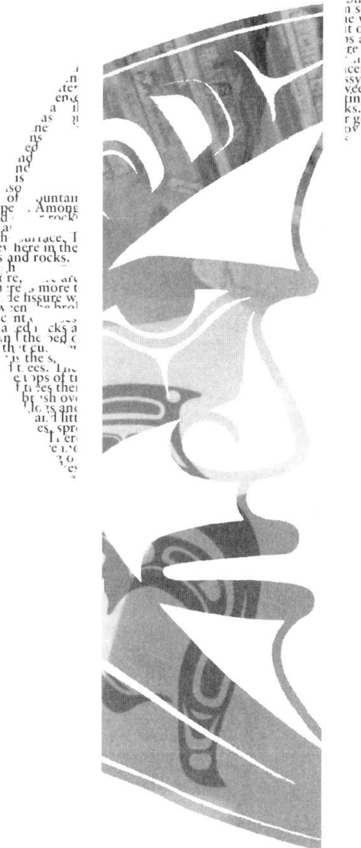

Notes

I remember getting drunk and falling through the streets. I remember not remembering the drugs. I remember passing out in the alleyways and waking up with blood on my face. I remember the endless pink and yellow acid nights. I remember smoking myself into the walls of some basement in some house. I remember being up for days. I remember drifting through semester after semester. I remember blacking out. I remember waking up on a couch in someone's house over and over. I remember the streets at night. I remember the emptiness. I remember trying to remember my name by digging out my ID. I remember acting only on the distant memories of instinct.

Notes

I remember meeting my Dad for the first time and asking him twenty-three years worth of questions. I can't remember most of what I asked him. I can't remember most of his answers. He wasn't what I had expected. I had always assumed that I had no expectations. But it turned out that wasn't true at all. I was disappointed that the hole in my life was still there after we met. I always thought it would go away. But I guess it's something that I carry with me everywhere now.

Excerpt from Exhibit "A" referred to in the affidavit

ORDER

IN THE PROVINCIAL COURT OF BRITISH COLUMBIA

THE APPLICATION of the applicant coming on for hearing this day; AND UPON HEARING M. Dunnaway, counsel for the applicant, Catherine Ann ABEL, and L. Thiessen, counsel for the respondent, Lawrence Melvin WILSON; AND UPON HEARING the submissions aforesaid; AND BY CONSENT;

THIS COURT ORDERS THAT the Order of His Honour Judge Gillis made the 24th day of March, 1987 be and the same is hereby varied

THIS COURT FURTHER ORDERS THAT the applicant, Catherine Ann ABEL, shall have interim sole custody and guardianship of the person of the child, namely, Jordan Skai Wilson ABEL, born April 13, 1985, until further Order of this Court;

THIS COURT FURTHER ORDERS THAT pursuant to Section 36.1 of the Family Relations Act, the respondent, Lawrence Melvin WILSON, shall not either directly or indirectly molest, annoy, harrass, communicate with or attempt to molest, annoy, harrass, or communicate with the applicant, Catherine Ann ABEL;

Excerpt from Exhibit "A" referred to in the affidavit

THIS COURT FURTHER ORDERS THAT the respondent, Lawrence Melvin WILSON, shall have supervised access of the said child;

THIS COURT FURTHER ORDERS THAT the respondent, Lawrence Melvin WILSON, shall have leave to apply to set aside the within Order on two (2) days notice of his intention to do so;

TAKE NOTICE THAT if you refuse or neglect to obey this Order you are liable to arrest by a peace officer and to imprisonment for contempt of Court or for committing an offence under Section 81 of the Family Relations Act.

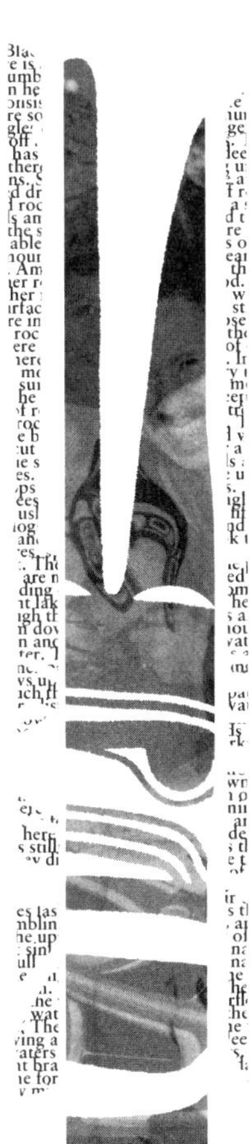

Excerpt from Exhibit "B" referred to in the affidavit

ORDER

IN THE PROVINCIAL COURT OF BRITISH COLUMBIA

THE APPLICATION of the applicant coming on for hearing this day; AND UPON HEARING M. Dunnaway, counsel for the applicant, Catherine Ann ABEL, and L. Thiessen, counsel for the respondent, Lawrence Melvin WILSON; AND UPON HEARING the evidence adduced and the submissions aforesaid;

THIS COURT ORDERS THAT the applicant, Catherine Ann ABEL, shall have sole custody and guardianship of the person of the child, namely, Jordan Skai Wilson ABEL, born April 13, 1985;

THIS COURT FURTHER ORDERS THAT the respondent, Lawrence Melvin WILSON, shall have access to the said child from 12:00 noon to 5:00 p.m. each and every Sunday commencing Sunday, May 24, 1987.

Notes

I remember standing next to the kitchen sink with a dull knife against my wrist. I don't recall exactly how I got there, but I was there. Pressing the blade against my wrist. Knowing it wouldn't be sharp enough. Crying and thinking about how much easier everything would be if I could just do it.

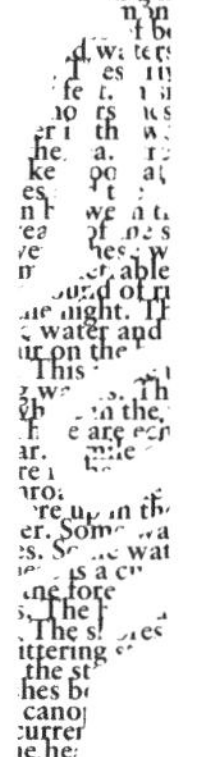

Excerpt from an audio recording of a presentation at the University of Saskatchewan

15:35:04	Here, I think, the lingering presence of Residential School violence is perhaps not explicit in all of my work.
15:35:24	In Sam McKegney's book, *Magic Weapons: Aboriginal Writers Remaking Community after Residential School*, he writes that "the Residential School haunts Native literature in Canada:
15:35:41	as subject matter, as setting, as repressed . . . memory, as source of anger, shame, pain, and violence,
15:35:57	and as unspoken backdrop to conditions of authorship. But it is nearly always *there*—
15:36:08	even when it isn't.
15:36:15	Residential Schooling has so marked the social [and] political . . . contexts out of which First Nations writers write . . .
15:36:31	that it persists as subtext to even those modern . . . works that [do not] speak of it explicitly.
15:36:45	It maintains a shadow presence,
15:36:56	an unspoken antagonism
15:37:03	that threatens community through its very silence."

15:37:12	I would suggest that one might read that shadow presence,
15:37:22	that silence,
15:37:25	and that haunting
15:37:32	into every moment in which an excerpt from Barbeau comes up in *The Place of Scraps*,
15:37:43	since those are also moments where I am attempting to grapple with my own experiences as an intergenerational survivor of Residential Schools.
15:38:01	Since these are moments in which I am forced to search for Indigenous knowledge through Marius Barbeau
15:38:14	because of the ways in which intergenerational trauma has impacted my ability to connect directly with members of my community.
15:38:28	What I'm suggesting here is that one can read these asymmetrical hinges, and the materiality of Barbeau's work, as attempts to represent
15:38:40	both the lived experiences of intergenerational trauma and the experiences of urban Indigenous people,
15:38:57	even though these readings are never made explicit in the work itself.

Excerpt from an audio recording of a presentation at the 2018 Digital Humanities Summer Institute conference at the University of Victoria

16:13:04 So, the shadow presence of Residential Schools came up for me in Andreae Callanan's essay "A Loss for Words" that focuses on my book, *Injun*. In the essay, Callanan describes the work as follows:

16:13:20 "*Injun* focuses on language,

16:13:25 on the loss of one's comfort with some words,

16:13:30 and the intrusion of others.

16:13:34 Abel's language may be pulled from early American pulp books, but the collection reads as a commentary on Canada's colonial projects—

16:13:51 namely the disruption, via the Residential School system, of the passage of Indigenous language and knowledge from generation to generation.

16:14:11 None of this is said, mind [you]:

16:14:17 there's no mention of Residential Schools,

16:14:22 or of the potlatch laws that suppressed the traditions of the Nisga'a Nation, of which Abel is a part."

16:14:39 Later, she goes on to describe her reading experience of the book:

16:14:54 "Here's what it looks like when I read the book:

16:15:05 I'm turning pages right to left by force of habit,

16:15:15 then righting my path by turning pages left to right while reading them right first,

16:15:20 then left.

16:15:24 The effect is almost slapstick;

16:15:31 the upside-down book is like some kind of dunce cap,

16:15:45 announcing that I don't know which way is up.

16:15:58 I may be an experienced reader of poetry,

16:16:07 but I look like a buffoon."

16:16:11 While Callanan does gesture towards the seriousness of the subject matter,

16:16:21 it seems as though she is confounded by a moment that seems to destabilize her reading practice

16:16:33 and her relationship to both Indigeneity and Canadian Residential School history.

16:16:45 Without getting too caught up in this moment, though, I think it's important to remember that this is,

16:17:01 one, a book that is dedicated to the Indigenous Peoples of the Americas;

16:17:12 two, a book meant to articulate and affirm Indigenous presence; and

16:17:23 three, I think importantly, a book not intended to shame settler readers for not knowing how to engage,

16:17:37 but rather a book that hopes to invite a dialogue about how this colonial writing has shaped and continues to shape us.

16:17:53 I think for me, this is where intersectionality needs to arrive. The moment where the reader turns the book upside-down and is asked to read both forwards and backwards, both up and down,

16:18:12 is also a moment where the reader is asked to understand and relate to an Indigenous experience and an experience of intergenerational trauma.

16:18:30 The moment that is missing here

16:18:39 is that conceptualism and text-mining, for me, are ways to work through issues in urban Indigenous identity and issues of intergenerational trauma

16:19:02 while at the same time providing a pathway to destabilizing and questioning settler-colonial canons.

16:19:16 To be fair, though, there have been a number of critics that have pointed to the inability of certain forms of conceptualisms to engage politically.

16:19:29 Take, for example, this alphabetized supercut of every single word in the first *Star Wars* movie.

16:19:41 Okay, or how about this predictive-text bot that is forced to watch over 1,000 hours of the *Saw* movies and then asked to write a *Saw* movie of its own.

16:19:59 Despite the fact that I really love both of these last projects,

16:20:10 I think it would be difficult to make an argument for their political and social relevance.

16:20:22 But I would also argue that the creative processes for both of these projects are not so different than the processes that went into creating my book *Injun*.

16:20:49 I think for me, one of the main differences is just the question *why?*

16:21:04 If we asked the other two creators, why *Star Wars*? Why *Saw*?

16:21:15 I think the answer might simply come down to fandom.

16:21:28 But when I get asked, "Why the western genre?"

16:21:38 my answer, as an intergenerational survivor of Residential Schools and as an urban Indigenous person,

16:21:51 is that the stereotypical images of Indigenous Peoples in the western genre were problematically some of my first images of Indigenous Peoples.

16:22:12 And my purpose here in this text is not to reinscribe racism,

16:22:19 but to dismantle it.

16:22:24 And to dismantle the colonial nostalgia that surrounds the western genre that so often goes undisrupted and/or unproblematized.

Notes

I remember standing in front of a totem pole at the Royal Ontario Museum and reading the informational plaque. This was the pole that was taken from my home community by Marius Barbeau, and the event of me standing in this place was a reunion of sorts. Except I'd never seen this pole before. I'd only read about it in books. But here I was with the pole that should have some place in my history, in my knowledge. Here I was with no words to explain how I was feeling. Here I was with the pole and the plaque.

Notes

I remember talking with a friend about Tomson Highway. I had asked her if she had heard about his position on Residential Schools. Tomson had recently told me that he had a great time at Residential School and didn't want to say anything bad about it. At the time, I didn't really say anything. There was too much to process there and I hadn't figured out how I felt about it yet, except that it had made me uneasy. "Yes," she said. "I guess he is a Residential School denier now." I asked her, then, how one reconciles that position with his artistic work, particularly *Kiss of the Fur Queen*. She paused for a moment and then said, "Well, who are we to say how he should or should not deal with trauma? Could his refusal to go down that path again not be a way in which one deals with trauma? And if it is, who are we to say that you can't deal with trauma that way? You can't tell anyone that."

Excerpt from a handwritten notebook by Catherine Abel

ACCESS
RECORD

Starting: Sunday May 24, 1987

Excerpt from a handwritten notebook by Catherine Abel

1. Sunday May 24, 1987

—I dropped Jordan off at L.W.'s parents' house on Knight Street at 9:00 a.m. and picked him up at 1:00 p.m.

Excerpt from a photocopy of a handwritten notebook by Catherine Abel

2. Sunday May 31, 1987

Called midweek—
—landlord? rent–Victoria? questioned access on Sunday, said he would call back
—I said I would plan to take Jordan to L.W. place unless I heard from him otherwise
—No calls until early Sun. morning 8:00 a.m. I was told he had to cancel because he had the flu. It was cool and rainy out.

Excerpt from a handwritten notebook by Catherine Abel

3. Sunday June 7

— weather is sunny and warm
no call during the week no message on recorder
I did not take Jordan to Lawrence's place
I left my house 10:00 a.m. Still no contact.

Excerpt from a handwritten notebook by Catherine Abel

4. Sunday June 14

* Marnie called: this week gone to court to "fix" order made previously—was sloppy and needed corrections. Called on Tuesday June 9—said she would call back later.

—Received a call on Thurs. June 11th on recorder that Detective Mike Miller had called in re: to L. Wilson (case 55?) 665-2255.

> * Friday June 12—Police looking for L. Wilson in regard to sex offence on 15 yr old girl said to keep in contact—may be only chance to get him is through me.
>
> call 665-2255 7:30–4:00 p.m. Mon–Fri
> call 911 emergency to get Detective Mike Miller at home—

Sat. 13th received a direct call from L.W. about 11:00 am. He said he was in the country (?) wouldn't say where—would have called re: last Sun. but "freaked" out—didn't have rent—was doing some carving in trade for rent $ back at apt. on Tues. (June 16) will contact me—

3276 W. 6th at Blenheim
2nd floor apt (F?)

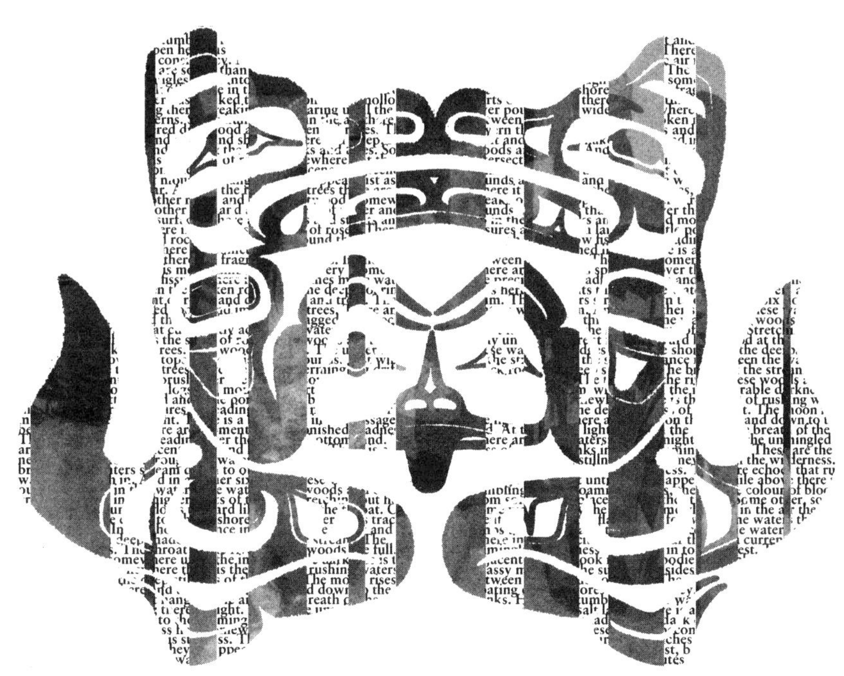

Excerpt from a handwritten notebook by Catherine Abel

—Mon. June 14th—I found out today the girl raped was █████'s older girl—█████—I felt heartsick about this. I am presently suffering a lot of stress & stomach ailments in regards to these events. I'm seeing Dr. Corbetti today for my "ulcer" problem. Talked to Marnie p.m.

Charges? Sec. 246 C.C. "Sexual Assault."

Excerpt from a handwritten notebook by Catherine Abel

Wed. June 17—Call from Lawrence on recorder "Just got back from Rock Creek—5:40 a.m. will call back later"

Fri. June 19—has not been arrested—interviewing—
warrant for arrest Mon. or Tues.

*438-4204 Det. Mike Miller for weekends
or call pager 667-5697
after 4:00 p.m. Fri.
if no answer call 911—

Sat. 2:20 p.m.
Knows that people are looking for him was crying—said he's going away for a while said he loved son Jordan a lot—was not long distance.

Wouldn't see Jordan this weekend

"will call back before he leaves"?

2:30—called pager for Det. Miller
5:00— " "
—gave message
L.W. left town.

Excerpt from a handwritten notebook by Catherine Abel

5. Sunday June 21, Father's Day

   no access takes place

Sat. 27th? time p.m.

L.W. called left msg. on machine

Hi this is L.

"Want to see Skai tomorrow."

No no. for you to call me tonite

Will call you tomorrow morning."

Excerpt from a handwritten notebook by Catherine Abel

6. Sunday 28th—Received no message on recorder from Lawrence —did not hear the phone ring—(went out to do laundry about 10:00 a.m.) No contact from him today.

Fri. July 3
665-2255 Detective Miller—(will call back after 2:00 p.m.)
* "Canada wide warrant—very unstable right now
"suicide"—"knife" ?

call police if seen—911 emergency

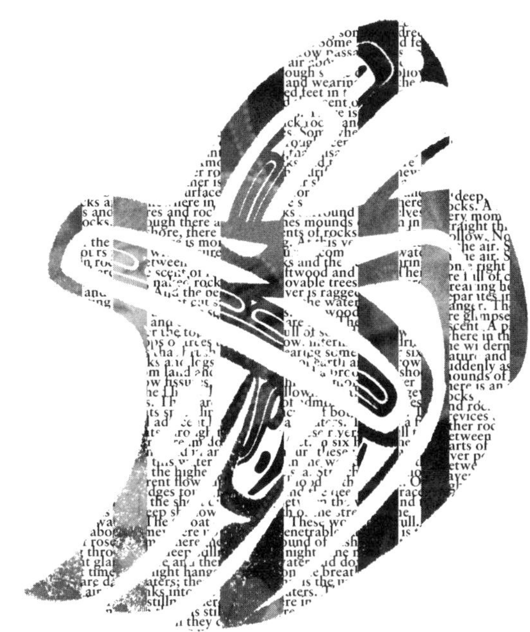

Excerpt from a handwritten notebook by Catherine Abel

7. Sunday July 5

Call from Marnie—

—evading arrest—not using access
—speak to detective *
make note for defence later

Mon. July 6

(circumstances—)
"charged but not guilty"—wait till found guilty
*suspended to court
<u>sexual assault</u>—3 levels of charge
—<u>minor level</u>

Excerpt from a handwritten notebook by Catherine Abel

8. Sunday July 12

——— NO CONTACT TO DATE ———

LEAVING PROVINCE ON

SEPT 2, 1987 for Ontario

REASONS 1) Family in Ontario—Mother Mississauga
—2 Sisters (T.O.)
2) JOB

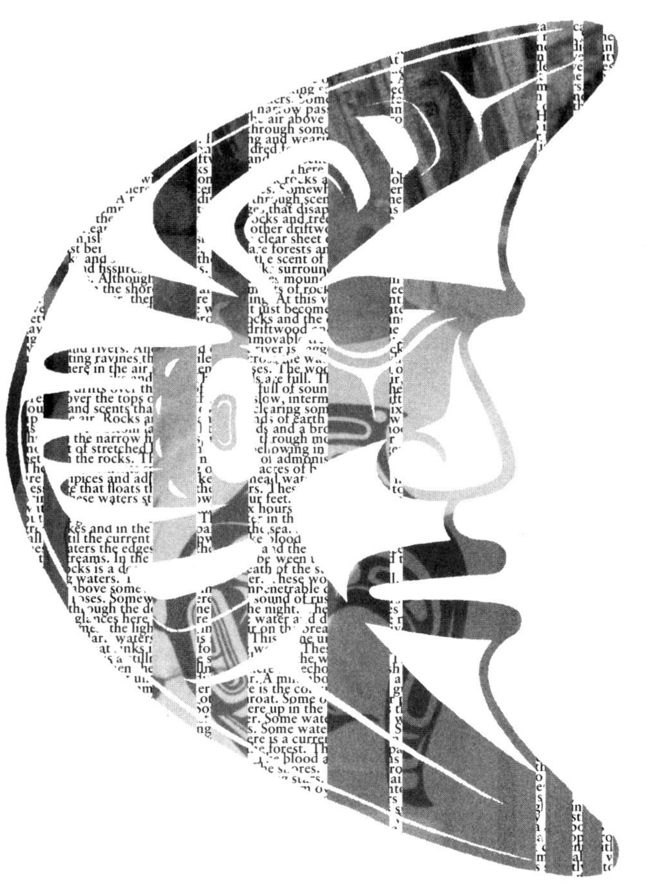

Notes

I remember talking with an in-law. For some reason we had started talking about Residential Schools even though I had tried to steer the conversation in any other direction. At some point, she turned to me and told me that her white, British mother had been to boarding schools as a child, and that it was hard on her but she got through it. So why can't we just get over Residential Schools?

Notes

I remember walking through Stanley Park on a beautiful summer afternoon, daydreaming about leaning against the railing of the Lion's Gate Bridge. I don't know what I would say or what I would do when I got up there. But it would be dark. Sometime between midnight and dawn. Hopefully it would be raining. Not because of the drama, but just because it's hard to see people in the rain at night in Vancouver. It's hard to see past your headlights. It's hard to see in front of you when you're looking at the pavement from under an umbrella. It's hard to notice people on the street when it's so easy to look past them. I don't know if I'd say something then. If I did say something, though, I guess it would be just for me.

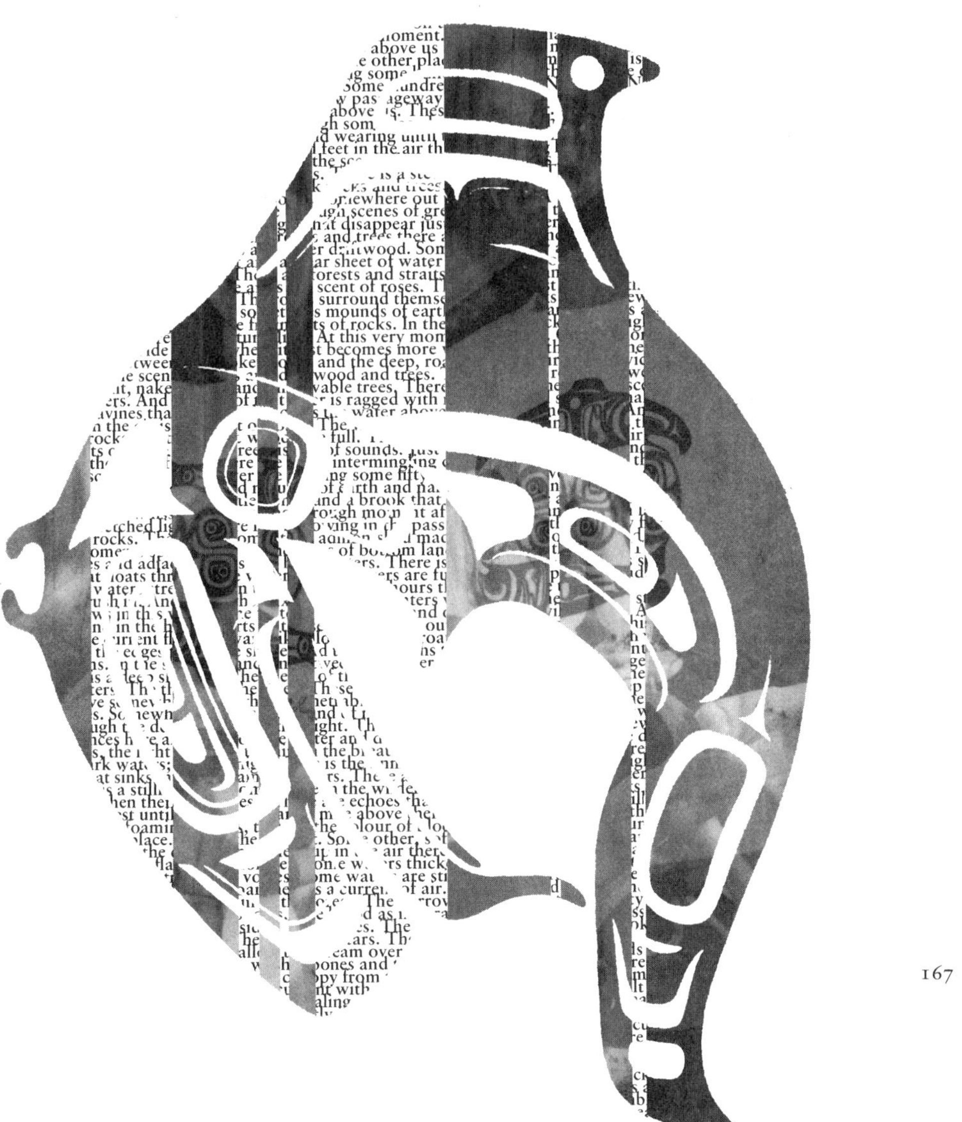

Excerpt from Nisga'a Enrolment and Ratification Application Form

Nisga'a Eligibility Criteria

You are entitled to be enrolled in the Nisga'a Final Agreement if you are:

> 1) of Nisga'a ancestry and your mother was born into one of the Nisga'a tribes; OR
>
> 2) a descendant of a person described in (1) or (3); OR
>
> 3) an adopted child of a person described in (1) or (2); OR
>
> 4) an Aboriginal person who is married to someone described in (1) (2) or (3) and has been adopted by one of the four Nisga'a tribes in accordance with Ayuukhl Nisga'a, that is, you have been accepted by a Nisga'a tribe, as a member of that tribe in the presence of witnesses from the other Nisga'a tribes at a settlement or stone moving feast.

Note: A person is "born into one of the Nisga'a tribes" if their mother was a Nisga'a.

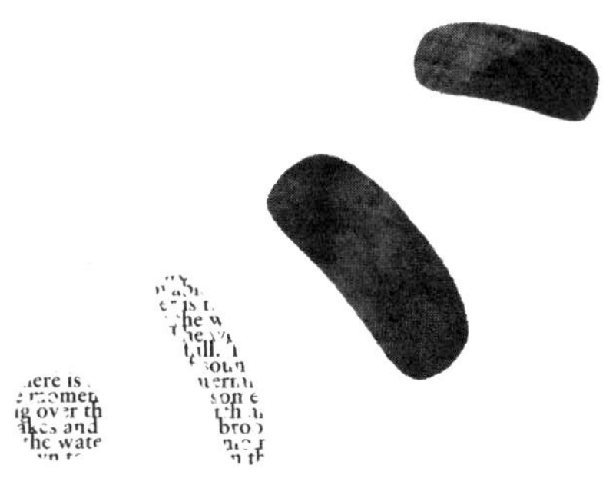

aring the
wo caverns. So
ere is attered drift
oses and roc a.
among t
of

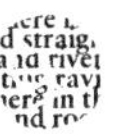

wearing there. Breaking and
into two caverns. Some hundred feet
here is scattered driftwood and the sce
npses of roses and rocks and shrubs. There
A path that winds among the black rocks
in the air there is the scent of roses. Somew
ilderness. A reasonable distance through sce
and glimpses of mountain ranges that disa
nly as they appear. Among the rocks and tr
ls of earth and other rocks and other drift
an islet and another islet and a clear
t beneath

beneath the surface. There are
and somewhere in the air is the sce
and fissures and rocks. The rocks surro
ocks. Although there are sometimes moun
n. On the shore, there are fragments of roc
of the river, there is more tumbling. At this v
ours into a wide fissure where it just become
n rocks. Between the broken rocks and the
there is the scent of roses and driftwood an
d straight, naked rocks and immovable tre
rivers. And the bed of that river is rag

in. And in another
grows in this water. The water
akes and in the higher parts of the sea.
ntil the current flows upward like blood
waters the edges touch the shores and the
streams. In the short distance in between t
rocks is a deep shadow. The breath of the s
ing waters. The throat of the river. These w
ng above somewhere up in the impenetrable
of roses. Somewhere there is the sound of r
through the deep stillness of the night.
on the water an

the light hangs in the
dark waters; there is night.
air that sinks into the foaming wate
st. There is a stillness here somewhere in
tning and then there is stillness. There are
ough the forest until they disappear. A mile
nbling. In the foaming waters, there is the c
m some other place. Some other throat. Som
ne waters carry the dead. Somewhere up in
nt of roses. Some flames last forever. Some
s and bodies and trembling voices. Some
in the velocity of the uproar there is a

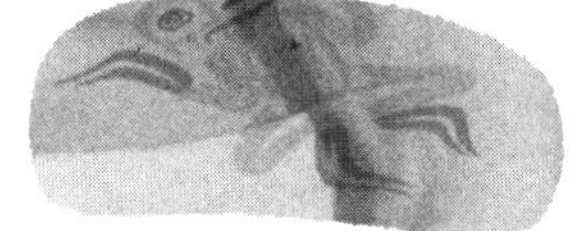

… it just be…
…en rocks and th…
…, and driftwood a…
and immovable tre…
… of that river is ragg…
…lently across the wat…
…ent of roses. The woo…
The woods are full. T…
of trees, is full of soun…
there are slow, interm…
…n over the clearing son…
…s and mounds of earth…
…d little ponds and a br…
… spreading through m…
There is a bellowing in…
…re moments of admoni…
…ng over the acres of bo…
…lakes and head waters.
…h the waters. These riv…
down to our feet. In si…
another six hours these…
…r. The water in the wo…
…r parts of the sea. Stret…
…upward like blood at t…
…n the shores and the de…
…listance in between the…
…v. The breath of the str…
…of the river. These woo…
… in the impenetrable d…
…re is the sound of rus…
…ess of the night. The…
…on the water and do…
…the air on the brea…
…ght. This is the …
…g waters.

Notes

I remember talking to my aunt Bonnie on the phone. At some point, she must have told me which Residential School my grandparents had gone to. But I had forgotten. That conversation just got harder and harder. I wanted to remember, but I didn't want to talk about it. I didn't know what to do with those details. So I ended up forgetting. When I asked her again years later, she told me it was the Coqualeetza school. After that, I looked up all the records that were available through the National Centre for Truth and Reconciliation. I remember searching through hundreds of photos with no way of knowing which anonymous child was my grandmother, which anonymous child was my grandfather.

Notes

I remember standing in front of a group of professors and students during a job interview. I had just finished telling them about my life, about my father, about the ways that I've experienced Indigeneity. At this point, I had done a few of these kinds of presentations, but they hadn't gotten any easier. They never got more comfortable. At the end of each one I often experienced a moment of regret. *I shouldn't have said anything. I shouldn't have put myself out there. I'm an idiot for making myself this vulnerable. I don't want to talk about any of this.* Sometimes this moment passes quickly and sometimes it doesn't. During the question period, a professor raised his hand, and spoke for several minutes before coming to his question: "What's new about this?" He didn't really care about how I might respond. He just wanted me to know that he didn't think my work had any value. I should have shrugged this off. But this question has stuck with me. If he asked me that now, I would say: "Nothing. This is an old, sad, painful story that hurts just as much yesterday as it does today. There's nothing new about it but it's still not going anywhere."

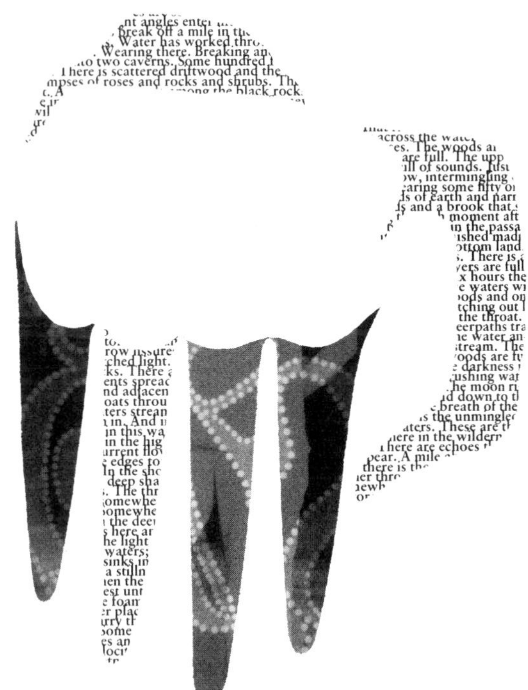

Excerpt from an audio recording of a presentation at the University of Windsor, 2018

10:07:45	The tone—in regards to the shadow presence of Residential Schools in my work,
10:07:57	and also to any lack of explicit details about the disruption of Indigenous knowledges—is,
10:08:09	I believe,
10:08:13	one of frustration.
10:08:17	However, I think it also productively steps towards answering Helen Hoy's question
10:08:26	—"How Should I Read These?"—
10:08:31	by connecting Indigenous history and the lived experiences of Indigenous Peoples back to contemporary Indigenous literature.
10:08:47	Here, I think works like *Monkey Beach* by Eden Robinson face similar challenges.
10:08:59	McKegney suggests that "even though Residential School transgressions appear to be at the core of the novel's contamination by violence,
10:09:14	they persist far more as an absence than a presence.
10:09:25	In a book of 374 pages, Residential School is discussed explicitly only a handful of times, and mainly in vague or speculative terms."

10:09:41 Still, I think, Hoy's question is one that scholars of Indigenous literatures return to again and again.

10:09:58 One of the more recent attempts to answer that question comes from Michelle Coupal.

10:10:10 In Coupal's essay in *Learn, Teach, Challenge: Approaching Indigenous Literatures*,

10:10:21 she argues that Indigenous literature can be thought of (and taught) "as a form of testimony."

10:10:35 Coupal posits that "although not all Indigenous literatures in Canada fall into the category of what [she] calls fictional testimony, [her] contention is that much of it does.

10:10:56 Indigenous fictional testimony is literature that gives evidence to the experiences of individuals or communities,

10:11:13 often with pedagogical, therapeutic, or activist impulses for a broad—

10:11:22 that is,

10:11:24 both Native and non-Native—reading public."

10:11:31 While Coupal's work on this subject mainly concentrates on novels,

10:11:42 I would argue that much of her work also applies to other genres like poetry, drama, and film

10:11:54 as long as the work "was written as a means to testify to the complexities, ambivalences, and contradictions of . . . [the] experiences [of Residential Schools]

10:12:16 and their legacies in an imaginative strategy to speak truth in ways that the fact-based, adversarial court system would not permit"

10:12:29 and also as a means of "articulating traumas without compromising . . . privacy."

10:12:40 Also, this is probably a good moment to say that work on and ideas about fictional forms of Residential School narratives have been articulated before Coupal

10:13:02 —I'm thinking specifically of Sam McKegney's work on "spectral identity" and "imaginative literary identity"

10:13:17 as focused respectively through Anthony Thrasher's autobiography *Thrasher: Skid Row Eskimo* and Tomson Highway's novel *Kiss of the Fur Queen*.

10:13:31 What Coupal brings to the table are her pedagogical arguments for teaching Indigenous literature as testimony,

10:13:45 and her discussion of the testimonial imaginary that focused on Robert Arthur Alexie's novel *Porcupines and China Dolls*.

10:13:58 Alexie, according to Coupal,

10:14:05 "seems to suggest that the public disclosure of trauma is as much an act of the imagination as healing,

10:14:21 and, more radically, perhaps he is suggesting that testimony should be a fantasy or can only be an act of the imagination."

10:14:36 Here, I think, is a good moment to pause again and talk about testimony.

10:14:47 In David Garneau's essay, "Imaginary Spaces of Conciliation and Reconciliation,"

10:14:58 Garneau suggests that the "testimony produced for the Truth and Reconciliation Commission (TRC) is constrained by non-Indigenous narratives of healing and closure;

10:15:18 by Western religious ideology;

10:15:26 by an emphasis on individuals over communities;

10:15:35 by the public display of victims but not perpetrators;

10:15:46 and by the degrading and corrupting influence of cash-for-testimony."

10:15:57 For Garneau, the boundaries of testimony have been rigidly shaped by the TRC to a point where it is clear that "not all stories are welcome."

10:16:15 But what is testimony?

10:16:19 What is testimony capable of?

10:16:25 What does testimony look like outside of the TRC's boundaries?

10:16:34 What kinds of testimonies are excluded because of these boundaries?

10:16:45 Garneau ultimately concludes that "if artistic and curatorial practices that are critical of this structure

10:17:00 or that emerge out of experiences and ways of working and being that cannot be accommodated or contained within the TRC's display mechanisms

10:17:21 are to find room for expression,

10:17:27 those spaces must be articulated outside of an assimilationist frame of mind."

10:17:38 If one aligns Garneau's thinking on testimony with Michelle Coupal's work on Alexie's *Porcupines and China Dolls*,

10:17:53 then the boundaries of what testimony is,

10:18:01 and/or the imaginative possibilities of what testimony might be,

10:18:09 become much more porous.

Excerpt from an audio recording of a presentation at Simon Fraser University, 2018

09:46:37 Coupal's conceptualization of Indigenous literature as testimony brings with it other questions, though.

09:46:52 And one of those questions might be

09:47:00 how one might witness Indigenous literature as testimony.

09:47:11 I'd like to turn to two definitions of witnessing that I think will be useful in thinking through this issue.

09:47:24 The first definition,

09:47:28 which can be found on the Truth and Reconciliation website,

09:47:38 defines witnessing in the following ways:

09:47:46 The term *witness* is in reference to the Aboriginal principle of witnessing,

09:47:57 which varies among First Nations, Métis, and Inuit Peoples.

09:48:08 Generally speaking, witnesses are called to be the keepers of history when an event of historic significance occurs.

09:48:23 Partly because of the oral traditions of Aboriginal Peoples,

09:48:34 but also to recognize the importance of conducting business and

09:48:45 building and maintaining relationships in person and face-to-face.

09:48:54 As David Gaertner points out,

09:48:59 "TRC witnesses are instructed to carry with them a living record of Residential Schools,

09:49:11 along with the emotional/cognitive impacts of receiving and holding such testimony."

09:49:20 Witnessing

09:49:23 in this context

09:49:26 is an embodied process

09:49:31 that places a tremendous responsibility on the witness to not only listen to and understand the testimony,

09:49:46 but also to carry it forward.

09:49:54 The next definition of witnessing,

09:50:02 which comes from Samantha Nock's essay, "Being a Witness:

09:50:11 The Importance of Protecting Indigenous Women's Stories,"

09:50:21 is more careful to unpack the nuances of witnessing.

09:50:31 “Too often,

09:50:34 we think that the act of listening

09:50:37 is equal

09:50:40 to the act of witnessing.

09:50:47 Listening is passive.

09:50:52 We can listen . . . while making to-do lists in our heads,

09:50:59 [while] thinking of what we are going to have for dinner,

09:51:08 or what we are going to say next.

09:51:15 When we witness a story, we are not only present physically,

09:51:26 but emotionally

09:51:29 and spiritually,

09:51:31 to hold this story in our hearts.

09:51:34

09:51:40

09:51:42 When someone tells us their story,

09:51:49 that story becomes a part of us.

09:51:57	When you witness someone's story . . .
09:52:01	you are carrying a part of that person with you now.
09:52:11	You have entered a very specific and powerful relationship
09:52:20	that exists between the storyteller
a09:52:23	and the witness."
09:52:26	Witnessing, then, demands our full attention physically,
09:52:31	emotionally,
09:52:33	and spiritually,
09:52:35	and ultimately connects the witness to the storyteller in a profound way.
09:52:46	Although the above definitions of witnessing capture part of the process,
09:52:55	much of the act of witnessing,
09:53:02	particularly as I've positioned it in relation to Indigenous literature,
09:53:13	leaves many questions I'd like to continue to think through.
09:53:21	For example, what does it look like to hold the story of Eden Robinson's novel, *Monkey Beach*, in our hearts?

09:53:36 What does it look like to carry forward a part of Jeff Barnaby's film, *Rhymes for Young Ghouls*?

09:53:49 What does it mean to become a living record for Louise Halfe's *Burning In This Midnight Dream*?

09:54:03 If Lisa Bird-Wilson's *The Red Files* is a gift of testimony, what gifts might I give in return?

09:54:14 What shapes do those gifts take?

09:54:22 I ask these questions because I think they are important,

09:54:30 and because I do not know yet what those answers might be.

09:54:41 I am wondering now too about the relationship

09:54:49 between Indigenous literature as testimony

09:54:56 and the field of conceptual poetics.

09:55:02 I wonder if the testimonial imaginary can encompass certain forms of conceptualism,

09:55:14 and likewise,

09:55:16 I wonder about the argument that Vanessa Place and Rob Fitterman make in their work, *Notes on Conceptualisms*,

09:55:29 that "conceptual writing is [ultimately] allegorical writing."

09:55:37 is that also the case for conceptual formations of Indigenous literary production?

09:55:47 Can the ideas that cannot be articulated directly,

09:55:55 that must be accessed through allegory and through conceptualism,

09:56:04 also be the shadow presence of Residential Schools?

Google how to kill yourself

All Videos Images News Shopping More Settings Tools

About 9,840,000 results (0.52 seconds)

Need Help - Canadian Association for Suicide Prevention
https://suicideprevention.ca/need-help/ ▾
... suicidal thoughts to **yourself**! Help is available for you, whether through a friend, therapist, or member of the clergy. Find someone you trust and let them know how bad things are. This can be your first step on the road to healing. Contact a crisis centre. Source: American Association for Suicidology, www.suicidology.org.
Ontario Crisis Centres · British Columbia Crisis Centres · Alberta Crisis Centres

The Best Way To Kill Yourself – Be Yourself
https://byrslf.co/the-best-way-to-kill-yourself-790f2c1035ac ▾
May 11, 2017 - My roommate's white bath towel was soaked in red blood. I'd just tried to **kill myself**. I was a freshman in college. I was alone in the suite I shared with three other guys. And I was tired. Luckily, I was too tired to do the job as I had intended. I had just enough energy to stop the bleeding and clean up most of ...

Painless Suicide Methods | Painless Ways to Die | A Depression ...
https://www.suicideforum.com/2016/03/27/painless-suicide-methods-pain-free-death/ ▾
Mar 27, 2016 - Maybe you hurt so badly you can't see past the pain to the truth. But you are wrong. There are no 'pain free' ways to die. There are especially no pain free ways to **kill yourself**. Not just the physical messy agony of suicide itself, which is never like it is in the movies or on tumblr, but also the emotional pain you ...

'I Googled how to kill myself' | Health24
www.health24.com/Medical/Depression/.../i-googled-how-to-kill-myself-20171120 ▾
Nov 20, 2017 - I found myself on Google. I typed: "**How to kill myself** and make it look like an accident". Google pulled up a large number of results, and quickly. Today, I just typed in those same words – Google spat out 937 000 results in 0.75 seconds. On the first page I read – "Making suicide look like an accident"; "what's ...

How to commit suicide. (How to kill yourself) - YouTube

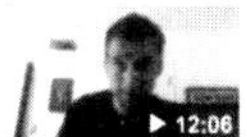

https://www.youtube.com/watch?v=g-K-6r0mSMA ▾
May 9, 2012 - Uploaded by KillTheFear
Definitely hate waking up and realizing I'm still alive. I've never liked life. Sure there have been happy ...

10 Easiest Painless Ways of Killing Yourselves Quickest - Insider ...
https://www.insidermonkey.com/.../7-easiest-painless-ways-of-killing-yourselves-quic... ▾
Jul 13, 2015 - For those willing to know, here are the 10 Easiest Painless Ways of Killing Yourselves Quickest. This article is strictly for those who are looking into ideas for a writing a short story. If you're really looking for ways to **kill yourself** please stop reading and see a shrink, or get high, or have awesome and ...

CASP ACPS Need Help Coping With Suicide Loss Understanding Get Invol

Thinking About Suicide?

Find Local Crisis Centres

- Alberta
- British Columbia
- Manitoba
- New Brunswick
- Newfoundland and Labrador
- Northwest Territories
- Nova Scotia
- Nunavut
- Ontario
- Prince Edward Island
- Quebec
- Saskatchewan

There are many crisis centres available 24 hours a day to ta

The last thing that most people expect is that they will run out of reasons to live. But if you are experiencing suici
alone. By some estimates, as many as one in six people will become seriously suicidal at some point in their lives.

Some Important Facts We Would Like to Share with You

Suicidal thinking is usually associated with problems that can be treated.

Clinical depression, anxiety disorders, chemical dependency, and other disorders produce profound emotional d
problem-solving. But you need to know that studies show that the vast majority of people who receive appropri
Even if you have received treatment before, you should know that different treatments work better for different
sometimes necessary before the right combination is found.

If you are unable to think of solutions other than suicide, it is not that solutions don't exist, only that you are curr

Therapists and counselors (and sometimes friends) can help you to see solutions that otherwise are not apparen

Suicidal crises are almost always temporary.

Although it might seem as if your unhappiness will never end, it is important to realize that crises are usually time
unexpected positive events occur. Suicide is sometimes referred to as "a permanent solution to a temporary prob
that will come your way when you allow more time to pass.

Problems are seldom as great as they appear at first glance.

Job loss, financial problems, loss of important people in our lives – all such stressful events can seem catastrophi
or years later, they usually look smaller and more manageable. Sometimes, imagining ourselves "five years down
that currently seems catastrophic will pass and that we will survive.

Are There Any Painless Suicide Methods?

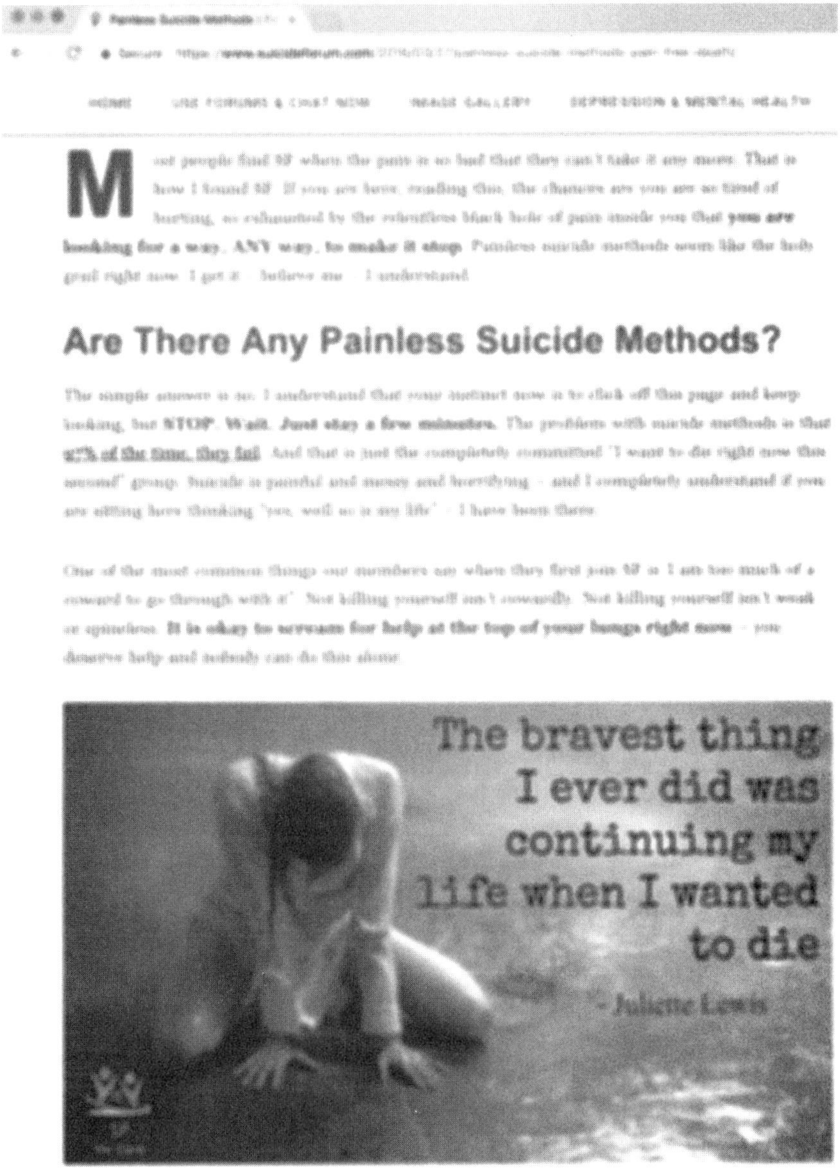

The bravest thing
I ever did was
continuing my
life when I wanted
to die
- Juliette Lewis

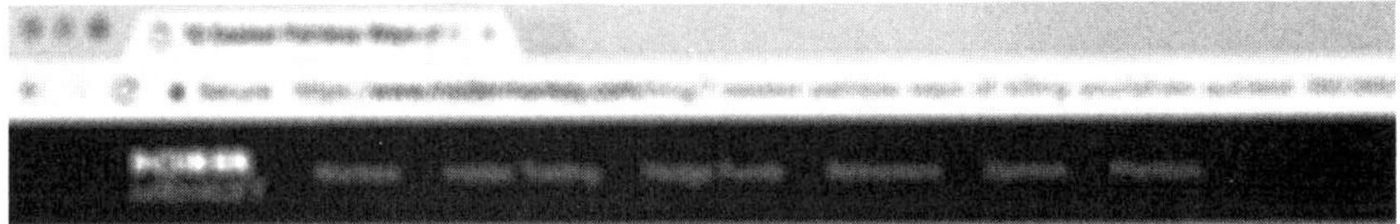

10 Easiest Painless Ways of Killing Yourselves Quickest
Looking for help?
Which is the largest pharmaceutical company by revenue in 2017?

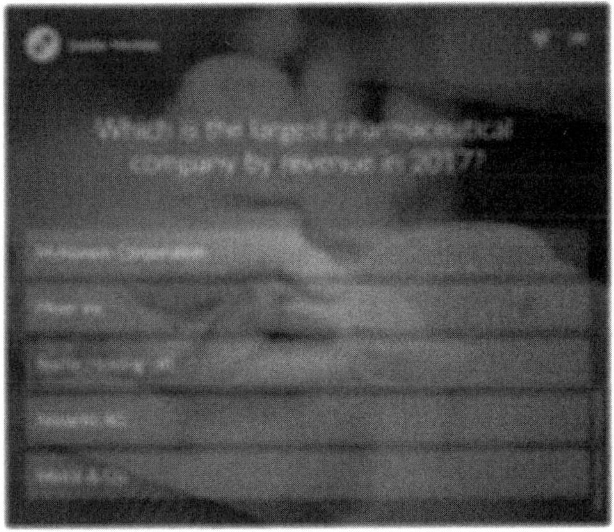

JAMES ALTUCHER
THERE'S NO PAINLESS WAY TO KILL YOURSELF

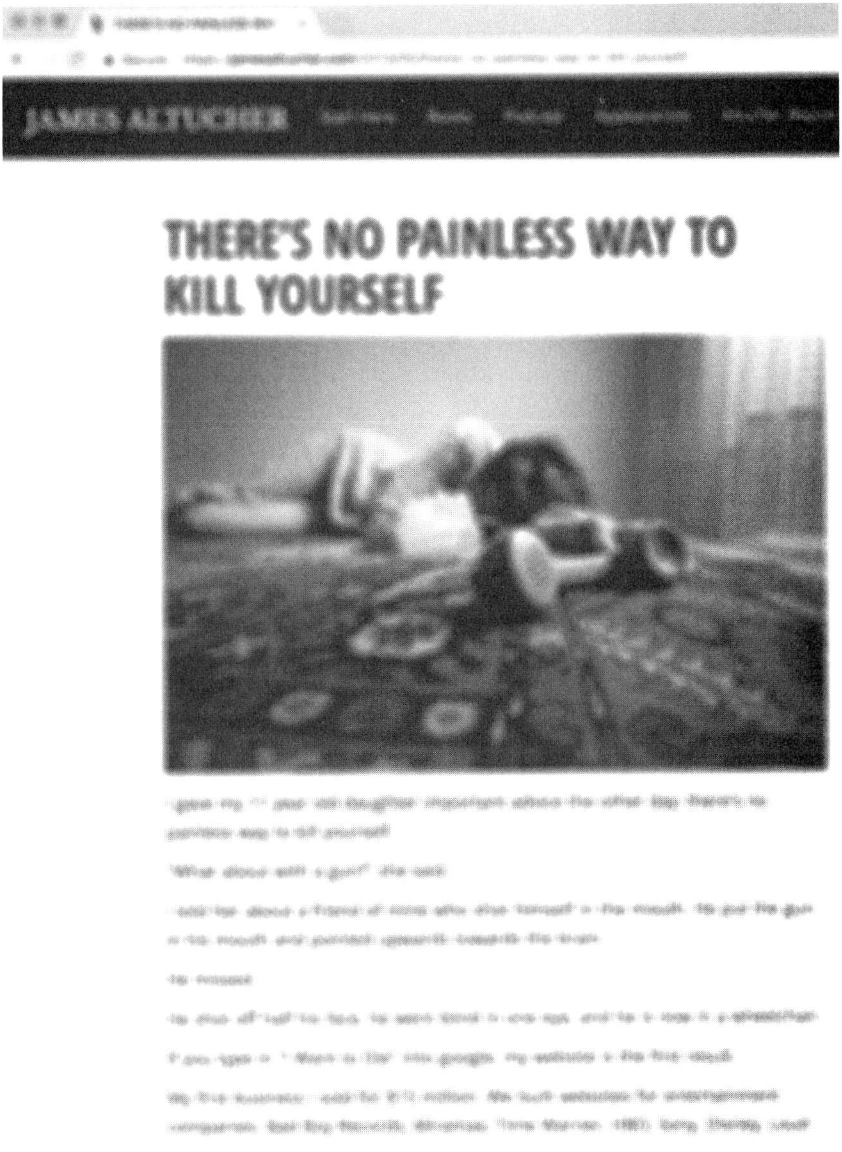

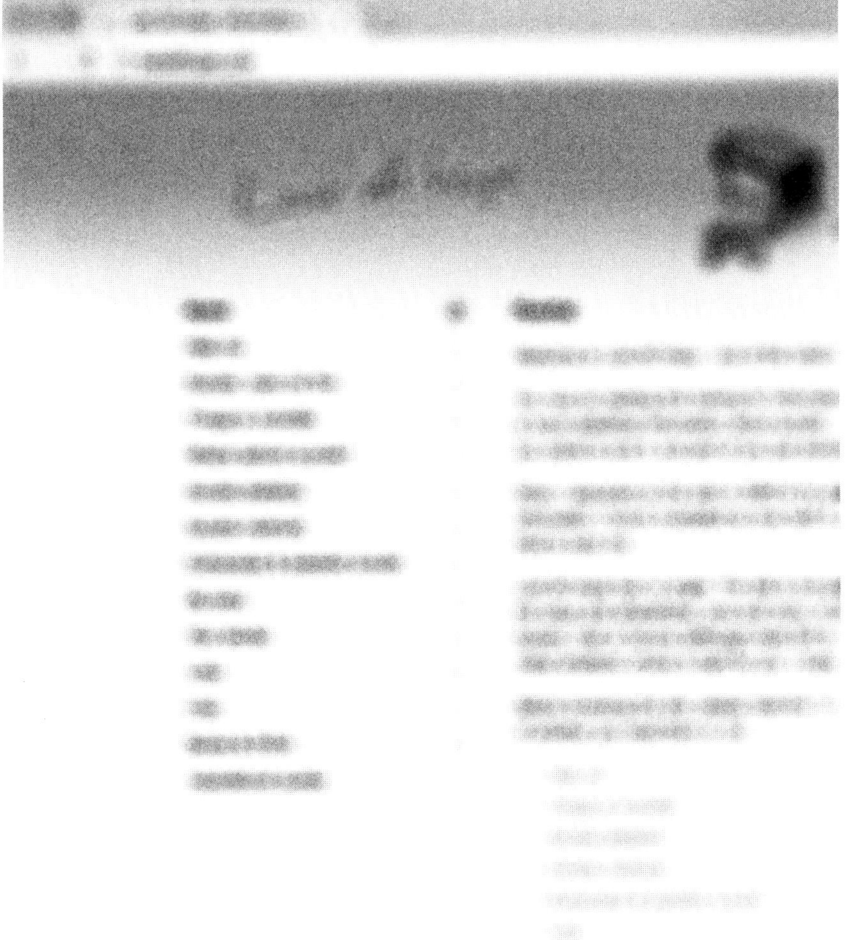

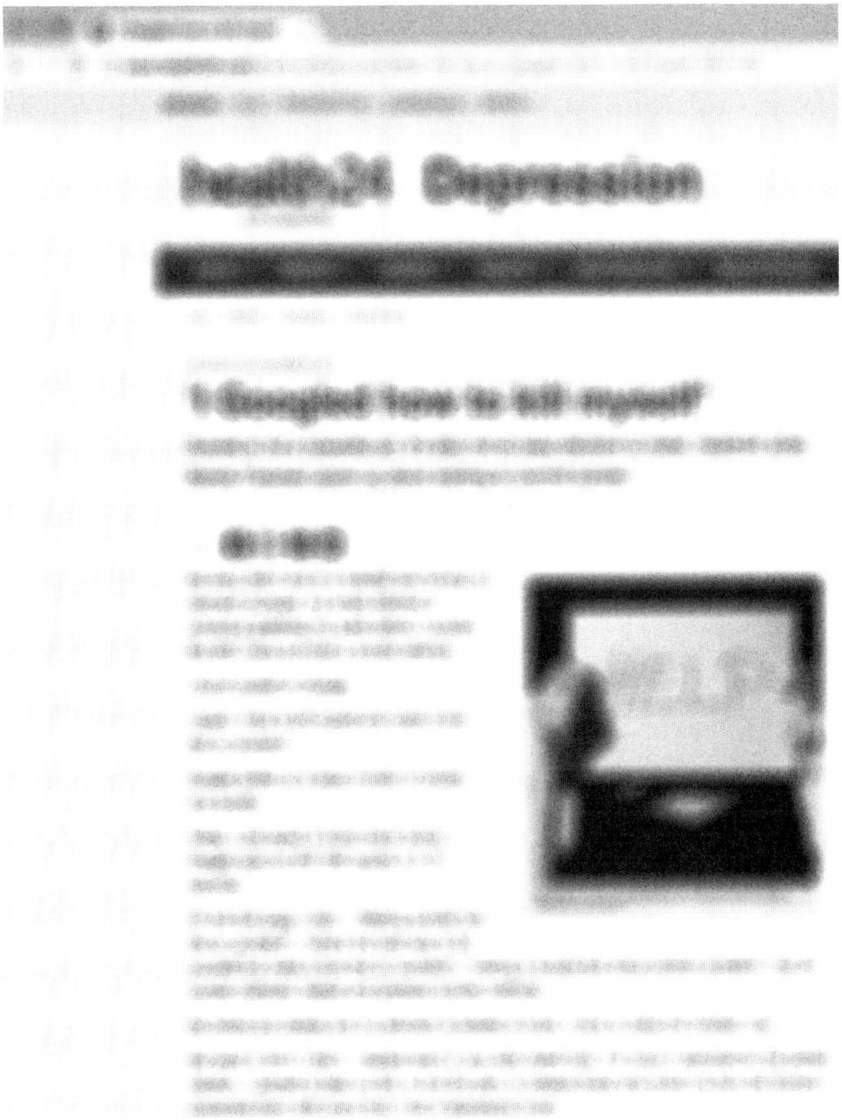
health24 Depression

OQUA-LEETZA
1893
USTRIAL INSTITUTE

COQUALEETZA INSTITUTE
THIS STONE WAS LAID BY
DUNCAN CAMPBELL SCOTT, LITT.D., F.R.S.C.
OF OTTAWA
ON JULY 28, 1923

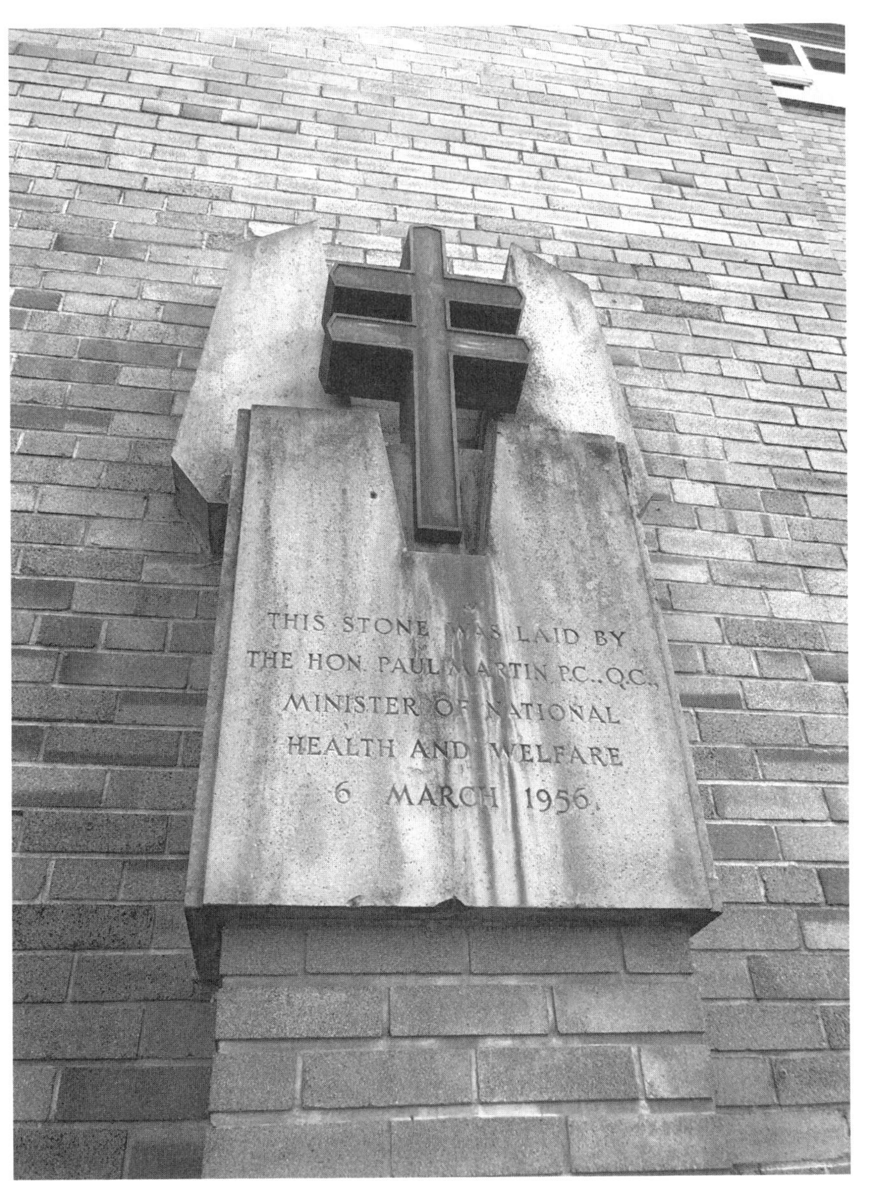
THIS STONE WAS LAID BY
THE HON. PAUL MARTIN P.C., Q.C.,
MINISTER OF NATIONAL
HEALTH AND WELFARE
6 MARCH 1956.

A deep, narrow chasm. Black rocks. The river lies still on those black rocks. A mile above there is a tumbling;
there is a moment. At this very moment there is a tumbling in the air a mile above us that runs straight through
the open heavens and into some other place. A deep hollow. No shape. No consistency. No breaking some
hundred feet in the air. Some places are softer than others. Some hundred feet up in the air. Some right angles
enter into narrow passageways and some right angles break off a mile in the air above us. These rocks are full
of cracks. Water has worked through some deep hollows. Breaking here. Wearing there. Breaking and wearing
until the chasm separates into two caverns. Some hundred feet in the air there is no danger. There is scattered
driftwood and the scent of roses. There are glimpses of roses and rocks and shrubs. There is a steep, rugged
ascent. A path that winds among the black rocks and trees. Somewhere in the air there is the scent of roses.
shore, there is the dark wooded outline of the forest. But which forest? Which shore? All the bodies can be
counted. Beyond the miles of water. Beyond the scattered driftwood. Beyond the scent of roses. There is another river. But that river is just more water between forests, rushing through the day. Every few yards, flesh
appears on the surface. There is light and bodies and straight, naked rocks and immovable trees. There is a
deep, narrow chasm. When the blood is hot, the current swells. When the blood is hot, the current sinks. When

Notes

I remember renting a car so that I could drive out to the Coqualeetza Residential School. So that I could finally stand in the place where my grandparents had stood. So I could finally be in the place that changed all our lives forever. But when I pulled up, I realized that I had been here before. A year ago. For a conference. I had stood here on the grounds where the Residential School used to be and not known it. I had been in this place before and not understood the role that it played in my life. I had even been here to talk about Indigenous literature and I hadn't felt it. I felt it now, though. I felt breathless and heartbroken to be here again. I felt like an idiot for not knowing last year. I remember I had gone to the first day of that conference but felt overwhelmed and burnt out. So I skipped out on the rest of the conference and drove in to Vancouver to live by the beach in a stranger's house for a few days.

Breaking and wearing until the chasm separates into two caverns. Some hundred feet in the air there is no
danger. There is scattered driftwood and the scent of roses. There are glimpses of roses and rocks and shrubs.
There is a steep, rugged ascent. A path that winds among the black rocks and trees. Somewhere in the air there
is the scent of roses. Somewhere out there is the wilderness. A reasonable distance through scenes of greenery
and nature and glimpses of mountain ranges that disappear just as suddenly as they appear. Among the rocks
and trees there are mounds of earth and other rocks and other driftwood. Somewhere there is an islet and
In the east, there are as many forests as there are trees. From flame. From voice. From the fire that sees itself.
From the rocks and trees. From the mounds of earth. From the driftwood. As the air flows down from somewhere deep in the forest there is silence again. No voice. No sound. There is a steep, rugged ascent and a path
turning through the rocks. There are flowers that bloom on the edge of the shore. Here the earth spreads from
south to north. There are clouds but only at a great distance. A mile above there is a tumbling. In the forest,
bodies glide between trees. At this very moment, the bodies pour out of the trees and just become more bodies
in the wide open daylight, spilling into the bright water. Beyond the flesh. Beyond the danger. Beyond the truth.
Somewhere between the ragged flesh and the treetops is the growing sound of voices. Voices speaking an unmingled sweetness that sinks into the forest. What trust. What coolness spreading through the beach. What
hazardous undertakings. In six hours these waters will rush up the shore. These water in the woods and on
the great lakes and in the higher parts of the sea. Beyond the horizon there are other bodies, other voices. The
sounds from the bodies drift through the air. For a few moments, the voices intermingle in the light that cuts
through the forest. Somewhere on the river, flesh can be seen floating along with the current. Behind the curvature of the shore, there is the dark wooded outline of the forest. But which forest? Which shore? All the
bodies can be counted. Beyond the miles of water. Beyond the scattered driftwood. Beyond the scent of roses.
There is another river. But that river is just more water between forests, rushing through the day. Every few
yards, flesh appears on the surface. There is light and bodies and straight, naked rocks and immovable trees.
There is a deep, narrow chasm. When the blood is hot, the current swells. When the blood is hot, the current

Notes

I remember walking around the grounds where the Coqualeetza school used to be and reading the small informational kiosks spread throughout. According to one of the kiosks, some of the children had carved their names and numbers into the wood underneath the porch of the big house. I wondered if my grandparents had carved their names into that wood. I wondered if they had carved their numbers.

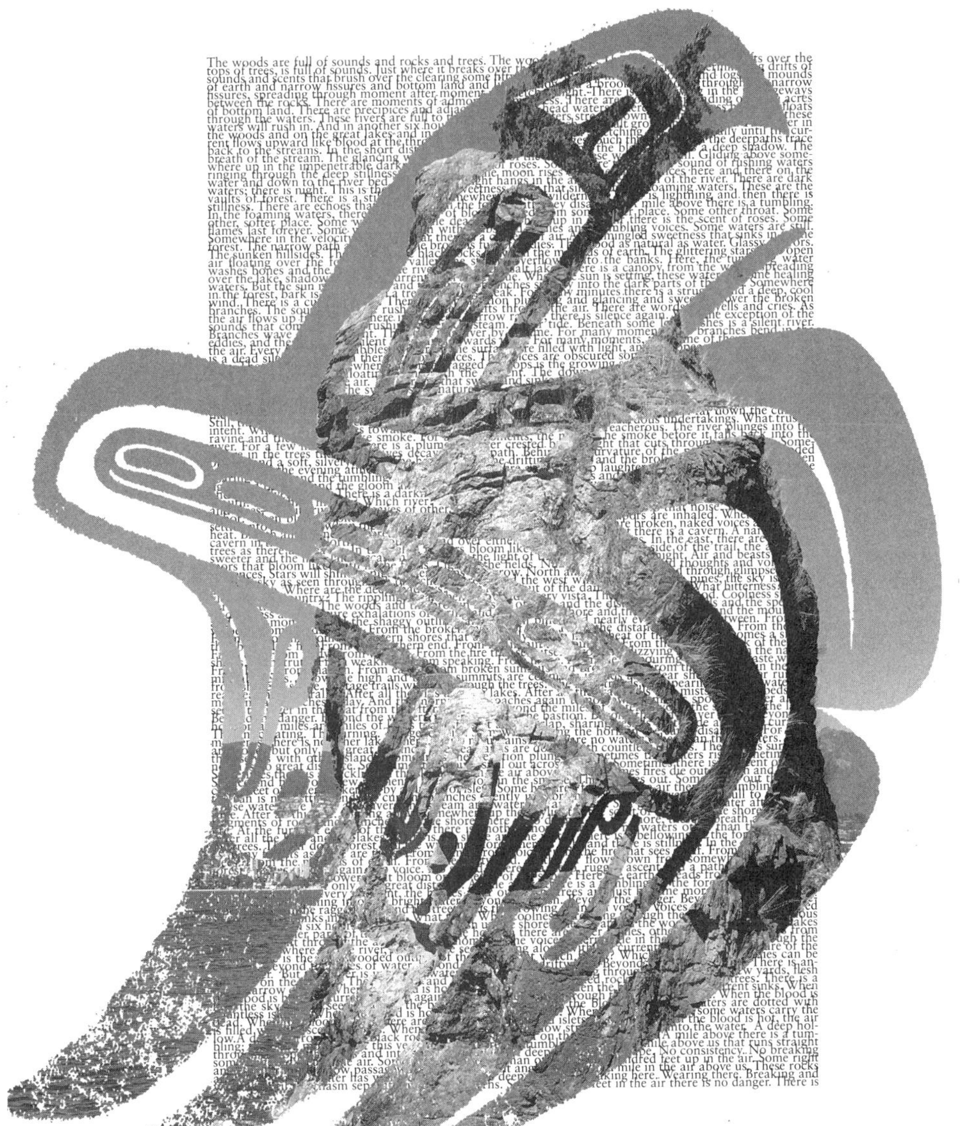

Notes

I remember standing in a daze on the Stó:lō territory where the Coqualeetza school used to be. I had spent so much time thinking about this. Thinking about how it might go. Where it was, what it would look like. I had arrived on a sweltering day at the end of July. I had been here before and I had felt momentarily like I knew this place. But I was also overwhelmed by that feeling.

I remember driving back to my friend's place just off Broadway Street. The sun was in my eyes. The air conditioning was on. I remember I was talking with Chelsea on the phone about what had just happened. About standing there in the same place where my grandparents had attended Residential School. I told her it made me feel weird and overwhelmed and strange. I didn't know what to make of it. I didn't know how to be in that space. I didn't know how to be back in that space. I didn't know how to feel about not knowing the first time. "I feel like such an idiot," I told her. "I should have known. I was just there. For some other reason. I should have only been there for one reason. But I wasn't. I should have known. But I didn't know." I told her it reminded me about the time that I had seen the totem pole in the Royal Ontario Museum as a child without knowing that I had a connection to that pole, that it had been stolen from my family's home community. I told her I was getting tired of having experiences like this.

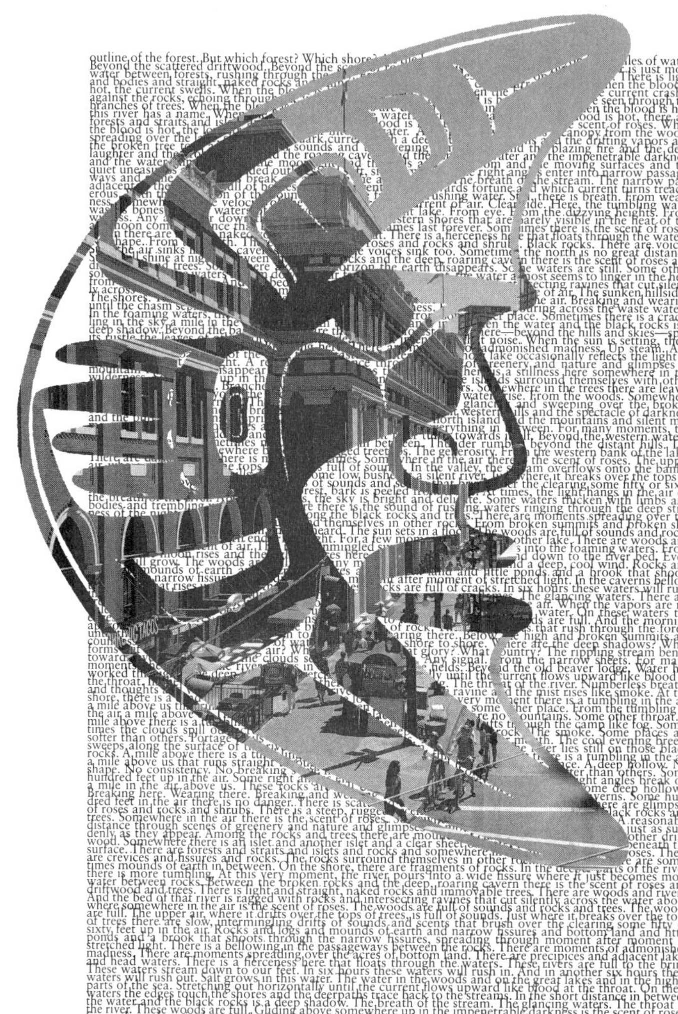
At this very moment, the river pours into a wide fissure where it just becomes more water between rocks. Between the broken rocks and the deep, roaring cavern there is the scent of roses and driftwood and trees. There is light and straight, naked rocks and immovable trees. There are woods and rivers. And the bed of that river is ragged with rocks and intersecting ravines that cut silently across the water above where somewhere in the air is the scent of roses. The woods are full of sounds and rocks and trees. The woods are full. The upper air, where it drifts over the tops of trees, is full of sounds. Just where it breaks over the tops of trees there are slow, intermingling drifts of sounds and scents that brush over the clearing some fifty or sixty feet up in the air. Rocks and logs and mounds of earth and narrow fissures and bottom land and little ponds and a brook that shoots through the narrow fissures, spreading through moment after moment of stretched light. There is a bellowing in the passageways between the rocks. There are moments of admonished madness. There are moments spreading over the acres of bottom land. There are precipices and adjacent lakes and head waters. There is a fierceness here that floats through the waters. These rivers are full to the brim. These waters stream down to our feet. In six hours these waters will rush in. And in another six hours these waters will rush out. Salt grows in this water. The water in the woods and on the great lakes and in the higher parts of the sea. Stretching out horizontally until the current flows upward like blood at the throat. On these waters the edges touch the shores and the deerpaths trace back to the streams. In the short distance in between the water and the black rocks is a deep shadow. The breath of the stream. The glancing waters. The throat of the river. These woods are full. Gliding above somewhere up in the impenetrable darkness is the scent of roses. Somewhere there is the sound of rushing waters ringing through the deep stillness of the night. The moon rises and the light glances here and there on the water and down to the river bed. At times, the light hangs in the air on the breath of the river. There are dark waters; there is night. This is the unmingled sweetness of air that sinks into the foaming waters. These are the vaults of forest. There is a stillness here somewhere in the wilderness. There is lightning and then there is stillness. There are echoes that rush through the forest until they disappear. A mile above there is a tumbling. In the foaming waters, there is the colour of blood gushed from some other place. Some other throat. Some other, softer place. Some waters carry the dead. Somewhere up in the air there is the scent of roses. Some flames last forever. Some waters thicken with limbs and bodies and trembling voices. Some waters are still. Somewhere in the velocity of the uproar there is a current of air. An unmingled sweetness that sinks in to the forest. The narrow path adjacent to the brook is full of bodies. The blood as natural as water. Glassy mirrors. The sunken hillsides. The shores. The black rocks between the

I remember about a year before I was here on Stó:lō territory for a conference about Indigenous literatures. I had been there to learn. I had a chance to catch up with friends. I talked with my supervisor about this book about intergenerational trauma that I was working on. I talked with a few people about how to apply for jobs, how to finish off a Ph.D., how to have balance in life. They gave me some good advice. That night I went for dinner with a few of my friends from the conference and ended up back in someone's hotel room with about eight other people. I remember someone drinking a glass of red wine from one of those individually wrapped little plastic cups that they put in hotel bathrooms. I remember laughing and talking and having a good time. A year later, I remember waking up in the parking lot of that hotel in my rental car just a few hundred metres away from where the Coqualeetza school had been. For a moment, I didn't realize where I was, and then I wondered how many times my grandparents had woken up here and felt that same thing.

outline of the forest. But which forest? Which shore? All the bodies can be counted. Beyond the miles of water. Beyond the scattered driftwood. Beyond the scent of roses. There is another river. But that river is just more water between forests, rushing through the day. Every few yards, flesh appears on the surface. There is light and bodies and straight, naked rocks and immovable trees. There is a deep, narrow chasm. When the blood is hot, the current swells. When the blood is hot, the current sinks. When the blood is hot, the current crashes against the rocks, echoing through the vaults of forest. When the blood is hot, the sky can be seen through the branches of trees. When the blood is hot, the waters are dotted with countless islands. When the blood is hot, this river has a name. When the blood is hot, some waters carry the dead. When the blood is hot, there are forests and straits and islets and rocks. When the blood is hot, the air is filled with the scent of roses. When the blood is hot, the low strands disappear into the water. A deep hollow. There is a canopy from the woods spreading over the lake, shadowing a dark current with a deep hue. The heavens and the drifting vapors and the broken tree tops and the sullen sounds and the evening atmosphere and the blazing fire and the deep laughter and the broken rocks and the roaring cavern and the tumbling water and the impenetrable darkness and the water glimmering in the moonlight and the hills and the gloom and the moving surfaces and the quiet uneasiness and the wooded outlines and soft, silvery wind. Some right angles enter into narrow passageways and some right angles break off a mile in the air above us. The breath of the stream. The narrow path adjacent to the brook is full of bodies. Which current glides towards fortune and which current turns treacherous. With the exception of the sounds that come from the rushing water. Still, there is breath. From weakness. Somewhere in the velocity of the uproar there is a current of air. Clear tide. Here, the tumbling water washes bones and the waters of the river go in to the salt lake. From eye. From the dizzying heights. From witness. Any alarm far down the current. From the western shores that are barely visible in the heat of the afternoon comes a silence that burns like fire. Some flames last forever. Sometimes there is the scent of roses. When there are broken, naked voices and intense heat. There is a fierceness here that floats through the waters. No shape. From the south. There are glimpses of roses and rocks and shrubs. Black rocks. There are voices. Still, the air sinks into the caverns below and the voices sink too. Sometimes the north is no great distance. Stars will shine at night. Between the broken rocks and the deep, roaring cavern there is the scent of roses and driftwood and trees. Somewhere along the horizon the earth disappears. Some waters are still. Some other, softer place. These waters stream down to our feet. From this spot, the water almost seems to linger in the heat from the afternoon sun. And the bed of that river is ragged with rocks and intersecting ravines that cut silently across the water above where somewhere in the air is the scent of roses. The rise of air. The sunken hillsides. The shores. The morning approaches today. No breaking some hundred feet in the air. Breaking and wearing until the chasm separates into two caverns. From the darkness. From the air pouring across the waste waters.

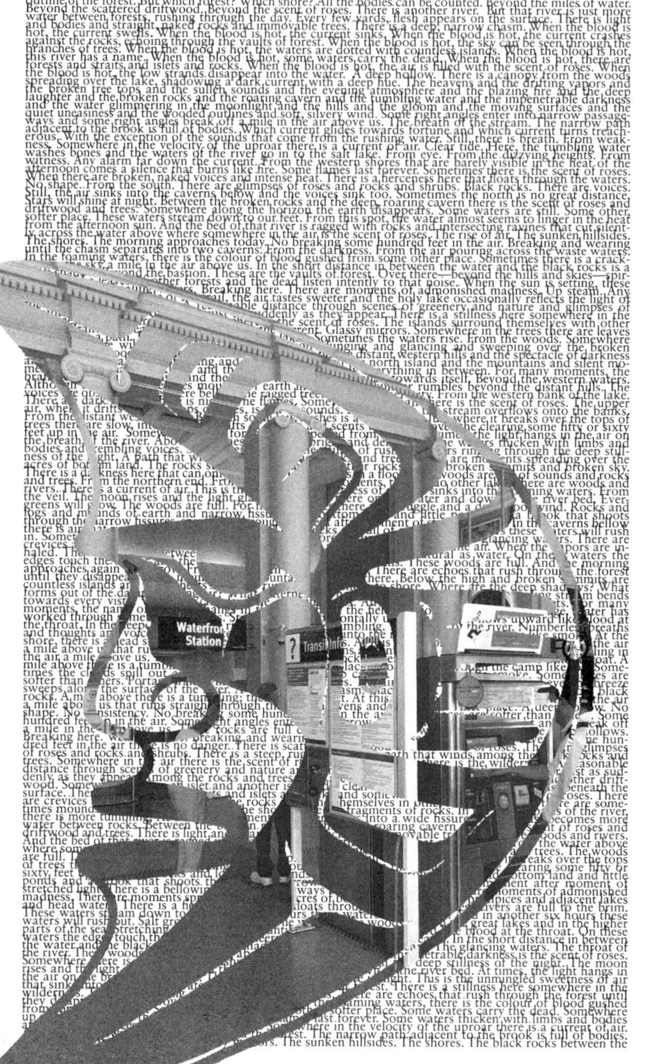

Notes

I remember hanging out on a patio with my friend Richard. I was drinking coffee without cream or sugar. I was telling him about this book I was working on. "It's mostly about intergenerational trauma and my parents and my grandparents, and a few of my aunts, uncles, and cousins." We talked for a while about other writers who had taken this journey, who had tried to speak honestly about their life experiences and their families. I told him that I wanted to write this book because it was a book I wish I had read earlier in my life. And that it was really meant to be for all of the Indigenous Peoples who have been dispossessed of their home communities and have complicated relationships with Indigeneity. I told him that it had been more difficult to write this book than any other book, and that I had wished I would have written anything else. That I had wanted to give up at so many points because it was just too hard to face some of these truths. He told me that it was important to come to terms with who we are, to accept the things we can't change, that growing up in our home communities and growing up speaking our language was a form of privilege, and that we shouldn't carry around that feeling of incompleteness. He said, "Jordan, I am looking forward to the day when you stop carrying around all that shame."

Excerpt from an audio recording of a presentation at a thesis examination at Simon Fraser University, 2019

09:07:35	Hey everyone.
09:07:38	Thank you so much for being here today.
09:07:41	The first thing that I want to say before we get into everything is that,
09:07:47	in the context of this defence,
09:07:50	this project is probably best thought of as a research-creation since it combines elements of creative non-fiction, found archival documentation, photography, concrete poetry, and academic inquiry.
09:08:05	I think there are probably a lot of things to say about what a research creation is
09:08:12	and/or what a research creation might be capable of,
09:08:17	but it may be useful to use one of Owen Chapman and Kim Sawchuk's definitions as a place to begin.
09:08:25	In their essay, "Research-Creation: Intervention, Analysis, and 'Family Resemblances,'"
09:08:34	Chapman and Sawchuk suggest that "research-creation may act as an innovative form of cultural analysis that troubles the book, the written essay, or the thesis, as the only valid means to express ideas [and] concepts,"

09:08:49	and that "research-creation can be read as a form of intervention into the 'regime of truth' of university-based research."
09:08:54	I should also say that I didn't set out to write a research-creation.
09:08:58	I just set out to write a book that was meaningful to me.
09:09:06	But I do believe that thinking through this project as a research-creation might help us address this project in this space.
09:09:17	Since the research-creation is very often about reorganizing, reframing, and repositioning research questions outside of the "normative frameworks for modes of presentation,"
09:09:29	I think it makes sense to readjust the defence accordingly, and to try to open up this space here for a dialogue instead of defaulting to the usual structures.
09:09:38	Okay.
09:09:40	So, for those of you who have been following my work or have heard me talk about my work over the last two years or so,
09:09:48	you'll probably know that I have been spending a lot of time talking about myself, my parents, my grandparents, and Residential Schools.
09:10:01	These talks have been pretty heavy to say the least

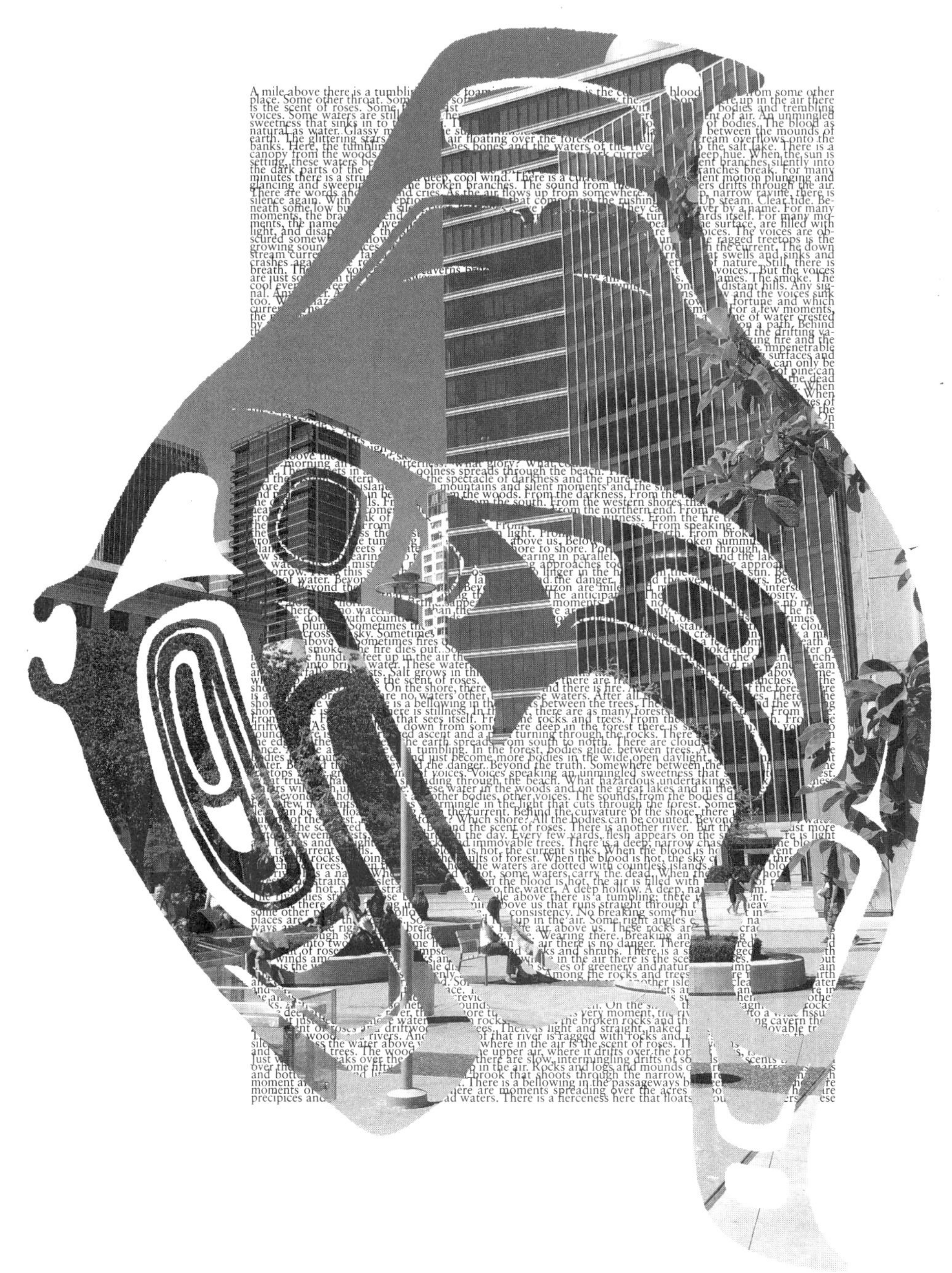

09:10:07 and have also been deeply personal.

09:10:11 And, in the spirit of truth and transparency, I have to say that they've also been incredibly difficult.

09:10:20 I feel like I need to say this because this work has come at a cost to me personally.

09:10:29 To be honest, I don't know how often I will be able to return to the work,

09:10:38 to talk about the work,

09:10:44 to engage with the work.

09:10:50 But I am here now.

09:10:53 In this moment.

09:10:56 And I wanted to begin this paper today by talking about where this project started.

09:11:05

09:11:07 A few years ago, I was in a graduate class on Métis Literature here at Simon Fraser University.

09:11:18 The class was taught by Professor Sophie McCall, and we ended up spending a lot of time talking about an article by Chris Andersen called "'I'm Métis, What's Your Excuse?': On the Optics and the Ethics of the Misrecognition of Métis in Canada."

09:11:35 In that article, Andersen asks the question

09:11:41	“What obligation, do any of us—Métis included—
09:11:47	owe dispossessed Indigenous individuals, and even communities,
09:11:53	who forward claims using a Métis identity based not on a connection to Métis national roots
09:12:02	but because it seems like the only possible option?
09:12:10	Whatever we imagine a fair response to look like, it must account for the fact that ‘Métis’ refers to a nation with membership codes that deserve to be respected.
09:12:21	We are not a soup kitchen for those disenfranchised by past and present Canadian Indian policy
09:12:32	and, as such, although we should sympathize with those who bear the brunt of this particular form of dispossession,
09:12:41	we cannot do so at the expense of eviscerating our identity.”
09:12:47	
09:12:48	I think it would be an understatement to say that this quote sparked something for me.
09:12:59	In fact, when I first read it, I had this overwhelming feeling

09:13:07 of both frustration and despair.

09:13:13 And it took me a little while to understand why.

09:13:20 It's not that I completely disagreed with what Andersen was saying exactly.

09:13:30 Actually, I find myself agreeing with him most of the time and I think his work on Métis nationalism and Indigenous Peoplehood is excellent.

09:13:41 The issue for me—and the thing that really frustrated me—was that this was just one more article in a long list of articles and books that seemed to be uninterested in addressing disenfranchised and dispossessed Indigenous Peoples.

09:13:54 On my part, I do think it was so completely unfair of me to ask for that from Andersen's writing.

09:14:04 In fact, it's probably unfair of me to ask for that from any article about Indigeneity that isn't specifically also about the issues of dispossession and displacement.

09:14:15 Likely, too, I think you can make the argument that if I really wanted to read about issues in Indigenous dispossession,

09:14:23 I should have just sought that out and gone elsewhere.

09:14:30 But I think it's also fair to say, though, that issues of Indigenous sovereignty and nationalism are everywhere—

09:14:39 and while I now know where to find writing about Indigenous dispossession,

09:14:48 including some wonderful collaborative work between Evelyn Peters and Chris Andersen—

09:14:56 many of those sources weren't visible to me at that time.

09:15:03 All I could see—

09:15:06 through the books I was reading, through the relationships I had,

09:15:13 through the communities I had access to—

09:15:20 was work that seemed to be disinterested in the very issues that I found to be the most compelling.

09:15:28

09:15:30 So I just wanted to start out this talk by saying this moment was actually a catalyzing moment for me,

09:15:41 and I think this project as a whole really grew out of this moment.

09:15:50 I also wanted to say that I am deeply grateful to Sophie for putting that article on the syllabus

09:16:00 and for all the formative conversations that we've had.

09:16:08 I should also say, for those of you in the audience, that this dissertation as a whole is now a book called *NISHGA*

09:16:19 that will be coming out in 2020 with McClelland & Stewart.

09:16:27 The book, of course, is really meant to function as a whole unit,

09:16:35 but for the purposes of this talk today,

09:16:40 I'd like to focus on one particular thread that appears throughout.

09:16:50 And while I realize that many of you haven't had a chance to read this book yet,

09:17:01 I am focusing on a few of the concrete sections which I believe can be discussed out of context.

09:17:11 So, hopefully this will make some sense to you.

09:17:18 So, I'd like to start out by addressing some of the work that appears as part of the periphery of this book:

09:17:26 a short text called *Empty Spaces*.

09:17:31 There are many moments when excerpts from *Empty Spaces* appear throughout the book as a whole.

09:17:40	Here, an excerpt appears towards the beginning of the book as part of this frog image [slide, page 113].
09:17:47	An excerpt also appears here [slide, page 122].
09:17:53	And here [slide, page 130].
09:17:59	And here [slide, page 172].
09:18:05	Finally, *Empty Spaces* appears here [slide, page 231] where it occupies the background of one of the final sections of the book.
09:18:15	But before I talk about *Empty Spaces* further, I'd like to read the initial section of this project for you
09:18:24	since reading this excerpt in its entirety, and as it appears on the page in the book, is actually quite difficult
09:18:33	since the text is often either partially or fully obscured.
09:18:38	
09:18:39	
09:18:41	"A deep, narrow chasm.
09:18:44	Black rocks.
09:18:48	The river lies still on those black rocks.
09:18:53	A mile above there is a tumbling;

Coolness spreads through the beach. The woods and the broken masses of rock and the distant western hills and the spectacle of darkness and the pure exhalations of spring and the western shore and the north island and the mountains and silent moments and the shaggy outlines and the tall pines and nearly everything in between. From the woods. From the darkness. From the broken masses of rock. From the distant western hills. From the veil. From the south. From the western shores that are barely visible in the heat of the afternoon comes a silence that burns like fire. From the northern end. From mountain to mountain. From the western bank of the lake. From eye. From body. From witness. From the fire that sees itself. From the dizzying heights. From the narrow sheets. From truth. From weakness. From speaking. From flame. From the air pouring across the waste waters. From light. From margin. From earth. From broken summits and broken sky. From the tumbling in the air a mile above us. Below the high and broken summits are countless islands and clear sheets of water running from shore to shore. Portage trails winding through the trees. The low strands disappearing into the water and reappearing in parallel. After all the hills and the lakes. After all the waterfalls and mists and riverbeds. The morning approaches today. And the morning approaches again tomorrow. From this spot, the water almost seems to linger in the heat from the afternoon sun. Beyond the miles of water. Beyond the shores of the lakes. Beyond the danger. Beyond the western waters. Beyond the bastion. Beyond the old beaver lodge. Beyond the horizon are miles and miles of lakes that intersect and overlap, sharing vessels that glide along the currents. The anticipating. The turning. The generosity. Somewhere along the horizon the earth disappears. For a few moments, there is no other lake. There are no mountains. There are no waters other than these waters. There are clouds but only at a great distance. The headlands are dotted with countless islands. The islands surround themselves with other islands. Sometimes the elevation plunges. Sometimes the waters rise. Sometimes the north is no great distance. Sometimes the clouds spill out across the sky. Sometimes there is the scent of roses. Sometimes there is a crackling in the sky a mile in the air above us. Sometimes fires die
woods spreading over the lake, shadowing a dark current with a deep hue. When the sun is setting, these waters become healing waters. But the sun is not setting and the current branches silently into the dark parts of the lake. Somewhere in the forest, bark is peeled from a tree. Branches break. For many minutes there is a struggle and a deep, cool wind. There is a current of air. There is silent motion plunging and glancing and sweeping over the broken branches. The sound from the rushing waters drifts through the air. There are words and yells and cries. As the air flows up from somewhere in the deep, narrow ravine, there is silence again. With the exception of the sounds that come from the rushing water. Up steam. Clear tide. Beneath some low bushes is a silent river. Branches wave in the current. They call this river by a name. For many moments, the branches bend in the eddies, and the arm of the silent river turns towards itself. For many moments, the name of the river hangs in the air. Every few yards, bubbles appear on the surface, are filled with light, and disappear. At the shore, there is a dead silence, and then there are low voices. The voices are obscured somewhere bellow the ragged treetops. The rise of air. Somewhere under the ragged treetops is the growing sound of voices. Somewhere on the river, bark can be seen floating along with the current. The down stream current. The far down current, sinking again beneath the air. The current that swells and sinks and crashes against the rocks, echoing through the vaults of forest and the sweetness of nature. Still, there is breath. There are voices. In the caverns bellow there is air that rises up to meet those voices. But the voices are just sounds in the woods, sweeping through the branches. The air. The sparks. The flames. The smoke. The cool evening breeze sweeps along the surface of the river. Thunder rumbles beyond the distant hills. Any signal. Any water. Any alarm far down the current. Still, the air sinks into the caverns below, and the voices sink too. What hazardous undertakings. What trusted intent. Which current glides towards fortune and which current turns treacherous. The river plunges into the ravine and the mist rises like smoke. For a few moments, the mist is the smoke before it falls back into the river. For a few moments, there is a plume of water crested by the light that cuts through the forest. Somewhere in the trees there are leaves decaying on a path. Behind the curvature of the path is a dark, wooded outline and a soft, silvery wind. The heavens and the drifting vapors and the broken tree tops and the sullen sounds and the evening atmosphere and the blazing fire and the deep laughter and the broken rocks and the roaring cavern and the tumbling water and the impenetrable darkness and the water glimmering in the moonlight and the hills and the gloom and the moving surfaces and the quiet uneasiness and the wooded outlines and soft, silvery wind. There is a darkness here that can only be heard. Another voice. Another river. Another mouth. But which mouth? Which river? All the knots of pine can be counted. Over there—be-

09:19:00 there is a moment.

09:19:04 At this very moment there is a tumbling in the air a mile above us that runs straight through the open heavens and into some other place.

09:19:17 A deep hollow.

09:19:19 No shape.

09:19:22 No consistency.

09:19:26 No breaking some hundred feet in the air.

09:19:32 Some places are softer than others.

09:19:38 Some hundred feet up in the air.

09:19:43 Some right angles enter into narrow passage-ways and some right angles break off a mile in the air above us.

09:19:52 These rocks are full of cracks.

09:19:56 Water has worked through some deep hollows.

09:20:03 Breaking here. Wearing there.

09:20:09 Breaking and wearing until the chasm separates into two caverns.

09:20:19 Some hundred feet in the air there is no danger.

09:20:27 There is scattered driftwood and the scent of roses.

09:20:35	There are glimpses of roses and rocks and shrubs.
09:20:44	There is a steep, rugged ascent.
09:20:51	A path that winds among the black rocks and trees.
09:20:59	Somewhere in the air there is the scent of roses.
09:21:07	Somewhere out there is the wilderness.
09:21:15	A reasonable distance
09:21:18	through scenes of greenery and nature and glimpses of mountain ranges that disappear just as suddenly as they appear.
09:21:29	Among the rocks and trees there are mounds of earth and other rocks and other driftwood.
09:21:40	Somewhere there is an islet
09:21:43	and another islet
09:21:45	and a clear sheet of water and bald rocks just beneath the surface.
09:21:55	There are forests and straits and islets and rocks
09:22:05	and somewhere in the air is the scent of roses.
09:22:14	There are crevices and fissures and rocks.
09:22:22	The rocks surround themselves in other rocks.

09:22:30 Although there are sometimes mounds of earth in between.

09:22:38 On the shore,

09:22:41 there are fragments of rocks.

09:22:45 In the deeper parts of the river,

09:22:49 there is more tumbling.

09:22:54 At this very moment,

09:22:58 the river pours into a wide fissure where it just becomes more water between rocks.

09:23:07 Between the broken rocks and the deep, roaring cavern there is the scent of roses and driftwood and trees.

09:23:18 There is light and straight, naked rocks and immovable trees.

09:23:26 There are woods and rivers.

09:23:30 And the bed of that river is ragged with rocks and intersecting ravines that cut silently across the water above where somewhere in the air is the scent of roses.

09:23:43 The woods are full of sounds and rocks and trees.

09:23:49 The woods are full.

09:23:55	The upper air, where it drifts over the tops of trees, is full of sounds.
09:24:03	Just where it breaks over the tops of trees there are slow, intermingling drifts of sounds and scents that brush over the clearing some fifty or sixty feet up in the air.
09:24:18	Rocks and logs and mounds of earth and narrow fissures and bottom land and little ponds and a brook that shoots through the narrow fissures, spreading through moment after moment of stretched light.
09:24:31	There is a bellowing in the passageways between the rocks.
09:24:36	There are moments of admonished madness.
09:24:41	There are moments spreading over the acres of bottom land.
09:24:48	There are precipices and adjacent lakes and head waters.
09:24:55	There is a fierceness here that floats through the waters.
09:25:04	These rivers are full to the brim.
09:25:09	These waters stream down to our feet.
09:25:15	In six hours these waters will rush in.
09:25:22	And in another six hours these waters will rush out.

The heavens and the drifting vapors and the broken tree tops and the sullen sounds and the evening atmo-
sphere and the blazing fire and the deep laughter and the broken rocks and the roaring cavern and the tumbling water and the impenetrable darkness and the water glimmering in the moonlight and the hills and the
is setting, these waters become healing waters. But the sun is not setting and the current branches silently into
the dark parts of the lake. Somewhere in the forest, bark is peeled from a tree. Branches break. For many
minutes there is a struggle and a deep, cool wind. There is a current of air. There is silent motion plunging and
glancing and sweeping over the broken branches. The sound from the rushing waters drifts through the air.
There are words and yells and cries. As the air flows up from somewhere in the deep, narrow ravine, there is
silence again. With the exception of the sounds that come from the rushing water. Up steam. Clear tide. Beneath some low bushes is a silent river. Branches wave in the current. They call this river by a name. For many

09:25:30	Salt grows in this water.
09:25:34	The water in the woods and on the great lakes and in the higher parts of the sea.
09:25:44	Stretching out horizontally until the current flows upward like blood at the throat.
09:25:55	On these waters the edges touch the shores and the deerpaths trace back to the streams.
09:26:07	In the short distance in between the water and the black rocks is a deep shadow.
09:26:15	The breath of the stream.
09:26:19	The glancing waters.
09:26:23	The throat of the river.
09:26:27	These woods are full.
09:26:32	Gliding above
09:26:34	somewhere up in the impenetrable darkness
09:26:39	is the scent of roses.
09:26:43	Somewhere there is the sound of rushing waters ringing through the deep stillness of the night.
09:26:52	The moon rises and the light glances here and there on the water and down to the river bed.
09:27:01	At times, the light hangs in the air on the breath of the river.

09:27:10 There are dark waters;

09:27:14 there is night.

09:27:18 This is the unmingled sweetness of air that sinks into the foaming waters.

09:27:28 These are the vaults of forest.

09:27:33 There is a stillness here somewhere in the wilderness.

09:27:39 There is lightning and then there is stillness.

09:27:44 There are echoes that rush through the forest until they disappear.

09:27:51 A mile above there is a tumbling.

09:27:56 In the foaming waters, there is the colour of blood gushed from some other place.

09:28:05 Some other throat.

09:28:08 Some other, softer place.

09:28:13 Some waters carry the dead.

09:28:17 Somewhere up in the air there is the scent of roses.

09:28:23 Some flames last forever.

09:28:27 Some waters thicken with limbs and bodies and trembling voices.

09:28:36 Some waters are still.

09:28:41	Somewhere in the velocity of the uproar there is a current of air.
09:28:51	An unmingled sweetness that sinks into the forest.
09:28:56	The narrow path adjacent to the brook is full of bodies.
09:29:03	The blood as natural as water.
09:29:07	Glassy mirrors. The sunken hillsides. The shores. The black rocks between the mounds of earth. The glittering stars. The open air floating over the forest.
09:29:13	In the valley, the stream overflows onto the banks.
09:29:20	Here, the tumbling water washes bones and the waters of the river go in to the salt lake.
09:29:31	There is a canopy from the woods spreading over the lake, shadowing a dark current with a deep hue.
09:29:42	When the sun is setting,
09:29:47	these waters become healing waters.
09:29:52	But the sun is not setting
09:29:56	and the current branches silently into the dark parts of the lake.
09:30:05	Somewhere in the forest,

09:30:10 bark is peeled from a tree.

09:30:14 Branches break.

09:30:17 For many minutes there is a struggle and a deep, cool wind.

09:30:23 There is a current of air.

09:30:27 There is silent motion plunging and glancing and sweeping over the broken branches.

09:30:37 The sound from the rushing waters drifts through the air.

09:30:44 There are words and yells and cries.

09:30:49 As the air flows up from somewhere in the deep, narrow ravine, there is silence again.

09:30:59 With the exception of the sounds that come from the rushing water."

09:31:06

09:31:07

09:31:08

09:31:09

09:31:10 A few years ago, I started a conceptual project that was connected to James Fenimore Cooper's 1826 text, *The Last of the Mohicans*. I initially became interested in Cooper's work after reading Roxanne Dunbar-Ortiz's book, *An Indigenous Peoples' History of the United States*, as part of a comprehensive exam at SFU.

09:31:32 In that book, Dunbar-Ortiz argues that *The Last of the Mohicans* plays an important role in reinventing the colonial origins of the United States,

09:31:43 and in creating a narrative that was "instrumental in nullifying guilt related to genocide."

09:31:53 Dunbar-Ortiz also argues that for the "generations of young white men" who read Cooper's work

09:32:04 "throughout the nineteenth century,"

09:32:08 *The Last of the Mohicans* and the rest of the Leatherstocking Tales

09:32:13 "became perceived fact, not fiction, and the basis for the coalescence of U.S. American nationalism."

09:32:23 After attempting to work with the novel in a few different conceptual modes,

09:32:31 and after failing to figure out how to make those attempts work,

09:32:39 I decided to do some additional reading.

09:32:45 I wanted to know who was reading *The Last of the Mohicans* today,

09:32:51 and what they thought of it.

09:32:55	Of course, one of the first places I ended up was Goodreads.
09:33:03	Turns out there are a lot of people still reading *The Last of the Mohicans* and many of them,
09:33:12	at least on Goodreads,
09:33:15	appear to be American high school students.
09:33:20	Also, it turns out they really hate it.
09:33:25	But they don't hate it for the same reasons I do.
09:33:30	Many of them appear to hate the book because they think James Fenimore Cooper is boring
09:33:41	
09:33:43	and they can't stand his seemingly endless descriptions of nature.
09:33:50	So, naturally,
09:33:52	I pulled out as many descriptions of land and nature as I could from *The Last of the Mohicans*
09:34:00	and I started writing over them, writing through them, writing around them, and writing with them.
09:34:12	*Empty Spaces*, at least as it begins,

Some right angles enter into narrow passageways and some right angles break off a mile in the air above us.
The breath of the stream. The narrow path adjacent to the brook is full of bodies. Which current glides towards fortune and which current turns treacherous. With the exception of the sounds that come from the
rushing water. Still, there is breath. From weakness. Somewhere in the velocity of the uproar there is a current
of air. Clear tide. Here, the tumbling water washes bones and the waters of the river go in to the salt lake.
From eye. From the dizzying heights. From witness. Any alarm far down the current. From the western shores
that are barely visible in the heat of the afternoon comes a silence that burns like fire. Some flames last forever. Sometimes there is the scent of roses. When there are broken, naked voices and intense heat. There is a
fierceness here that floats through the waters. No shape. From the south. There are glimpses of roses and rocks
and shrubs. Black rocks. There are voices. Still, the air sinks into the caverns below and the voices sink too.
Sometimes the north is no great distance. Stars will shine at night. Between the broken rocks and the deep,
roaring cavern there is the scent of roses and driftwood and trees. Somewhere along the horizon the earth
disappears. Some waters are still. Some other, softer place. These waters stream down to our feet. From this
spot, the water almost seems to linger in the heat from the afternoon sun. And the bed of that river is ragged
with rocks and intersecting ravines that cut silently across the water above where somewhere in the air is the
scent of roses. The rise of air. The sunken hillsides. The shores. The morning approaches today. No breaking
some hundred feet in the air. Breaking and wearing until the chasm separates into two caverns. From the
darkness. From the air pouring across the waste waters. In the foaming waters, there is the colour of blood
gushed from some other place. Sometimes there is a crackling in the sky a mile in the air above us. In the short
distance in between the water and the black rocks is a deep shadow. Beyond the bastion. These are the vaults
of forest. Over there—beyond the hills and skies—spirits rustle the leaves of other forests and the dead listen
An unmingled sweetness that sinks in to the forest. The narrow path adjacent to the brook is full of bodies.
The blood as natural as water. Glassy mirrors. The sunken hillsides. The shores. The black rocks between the
mounds of earth. The glittering stars. The open air floating over the forest. In the valley, the stream overflows
onto the banks. Here, the tumbling water washes bones and the waters of the river go in to the salt lake. There
is a canopy from the woods spreading over the lake, shadowing a dark current with a deep hue. When the sun
is setting, these waters become healing waters. But the sun is not setting and the current branches silently into
the dark parts of the lake. Somewhere in the forest, bark is peeled from a tree. Branches break. For many
minutes there is a struggle and a deep, cool wind. There is a current of air. There is silent motion plunging and
glancing and sweeping over the broken branches. The sound from the rushing waters drifts through the air.
There are words and yells and cries. As the air flows up from somewhere in the deep, narrow ravine, there is
silence again. With the exception of the sounds that come from the rushing water. Up steam. Clear tide. Beneath some low bushes is a silent river. Branches wave in the current. They call this river by a name. For many
moments, the branches bend in the eddies, and the arm of the silent river turns towards itself. For many moments, the name of the river hangs in the air. Every few yards, bubbles appear on the surface, are filled with
light, and disappear. At the shore, there is a dead silence, and then there are low voices. The voices are obscured somewhere bellow the ragged treetops. The rise of air. Somewhere under the ragged treetops is the
growing sound of voices. Somewhere on the river, bark can be seen floating along with the current. The down

09:34:17 is an impurely conceptual project that both animates and reanimates Cooper's representation of land as *terra nullius*,

09:34:28 but also calls into question my relationships —plural—to the land.

09:34:35 In *Empty Spaces*, the land is described in concrete details.

09:34:39 There are hundreds of specific images that operate both individually and as pieces of a whole.

09:34:45 But they are part of an impossible whole.

09:34:49 The land, here, is ultimately a work of imagination, appropriation, and transformation.

09:34:55 As I reflect on this project, I often wonder what it means that I am writing a project about imagining land

09:35:02 when my own relationship to Nisga'a territory,

09:35:05 as it's addressed in this book,

09:35:08 is deeply fraught.

09:35:10 Is it possible that my deepest connection to land comes through text?

09:35:16 Through imagination?

09:35:18 Through fiction?

09:35:20	If I've learned anything from Indigenous nationalism,
09:35:24	my relationship to the land should have been formed through a connection to the land itself,
09:35:29	through family,
09:35:31	through community,
09:35:33	through Nisga'a knowledge,
09:35:35	Nisga'a language,
09:35:37	and Nisga'a worldviews.
09:35:39	But how do those who have been dispossessed and severed from the land begin to think through what land means to them?
09:35:44	*Empty Spaces*, then, is not so much about re-presenting James Fenimore Cooper's vision of land as *terra nullius*
09:35:50	but instead it is about overwriting *terra nullius*.
09:35:54	It is about imagining and reconstituting my relationship with the land.
09:35:58	Much like many of my other projects, *Empty Spaces* is not so much about reinscribing Indigenous absence
09:36:05	as it is about rearticulating Indigenous presence.

09:36:09 So *Empty Spaces* is a project that is in part about these questions,

09:36:13 but it is also a separate project.

09:36:15 It's a project that has its own trajectory,

09:36:19 which may or may not ever find a conclusion;

09:36:23 and it is one of many currently unfinished examples of my personal artistic production.

09:36:28 I wanted to initially address *Empty Spaces* as a separate project, so that I can talk about how and why it appears in the book *NISHGA*.

09:36:34

09:36:35 There was a moment during the early stages of writing this book where it was important to me to put my own work in dialogue with my Dad's work.

09:36:45 There was a moment where I wanted both of our artistic trajectories to speak to each other,

09:36:50 to coexist together.

09:36:52 Perhaps I was interested in creating these moments because there were no equivalent moments in our lives.

09:36:58 Our works speak to each other even when we do not.

09:37:04 The moments that are here on these pages are ultimately moments where both of our artistic outputs intertwine and bridge a seemingly insurmountable gap between us.

09:37:13 Each moment, though, has a different point (or perhaps points) of intersection.

09:37:19 [slide, page 231]

09:37:20 Take, for example, this moment that appears towards the end of *NISHGA*.

09:37:25 My work here occupies both the foreground and the background.

09:37:29 The photo—which is literally shaped by my father's artwork—was taken last year in front of the Vancouver Art Gallery.

09:37:36 The photo, for me, is in dialogue with another photo.

09:37:40 That photo, which unfortunately is no longer available to me, featured my Dad and I standing in front of these exact stairs during the summer of 2008

09:37:49 on the occasion of our first and only meeting.

09:37:53 The photo on this page—taken a decade later —contains neither of us, but this page as a whole contains both of us.

09:38:00 *Empty Spaces*, here, is either the textured background that stands in contrast with the photo image of the frog,

09:38:07 or it is the primary text of the page that has become partially eclipsed by the photo image of the frog.

09:38:14 This moment, for me, is similar structurally to some of the symmetrical hinges that appear in *The Place of Scraps*,

09:38:20 in that there is a distinct point of transition between two directions of reading.

09:38:26 Here, that transition point is the space in between the work shaped by my father's art and my own personal work.

09:38:35 In some ways, our work here bleeds together,

09:38:39 and in other ways remains separate.

09:38:43

09:38:44

09:38:45 I do wonder what it means for my work to exist in both the foreground and the background.

09:38:52 I wonder what it means that I have gotten to know my father's art better than I've gotten to know my father.

09:39:00

09:39:01

09:39:02 I wonder how much you can get to know someone through their art.

09:39:07	I wonder what it means to be absent from this page.
09:39:10	
09:39:11	I wonder what it means to be present on this page.
09:39:15	
09:39:16	
09:39:17	Before I wrote *The Place of Scraps*, I had this feeling that my work was always going to end up going in this direction.
09:39:24	I knew at some point that I would need to write something.
09:39:29	Even if it was just for me.
09:39:31	But I had also hoped that this moment would never arrive.
09:39:35	
09:39:36	
09:39:37	There was a moment in the early stages of the writing process for this book where I felt like I could learn more about my father,
09:39:44	learn more about my grandparents,
09:39:47	learn more about my family and my culture and my language.

09:39:52	But those things didn't happen in the same way that I had originally imagined.
09:39:57	
09:39:58	I wish I had known my grandparents.
09:40:01	
09:40:02	There are so many things that I would like to tell them.
09:40:07	There are so many things that I would hope they would tell me.
09:40:12	
09:40:13	
09:40:14	But that is not possible any more.
09:40:18	
09:40:19	
09:40:20	When I started writing this book,
09:40:23	I did it just for me.
09:40:26	I did it so that I could hold all the pieces up and see how they connected together.
09:40:33	I also wrote this book because I thought I could write my way home.
09:40:39	I thought doing a project like this would bring me closer to something;

09:40:45 would bring me closer to knowing all the things that I don't know or that I couldn't know.

09:40:52

09:40:53 It turns out that wasn't the case.

09:40:54

09:40:55

09:40:56 I wish I had come to different conclusions. Different realizations.

09:41:01 But I didn't.

09:41:03

09:41:04

09:41:05 I came to the same conclusions and realizations that are here on the pages of this book.

09:41:10 I didn't find my way home.

09:41:13 I didn't find my way anywhere but deeper.

09:41:16

09:41:17 If there was a hole I was in, I just kept digging down.

09:41:22 But now that I've come to the end of this project,

09:41:26 my hope for this work is that someone else will read it and feel like they're not alone.

09:41:42 My hope is that the things I have written down here are helpful to someone.

09:41:51 This story did not turn out the way I had hoped.

09:42:12 I wish I had different experiences that led to different places and that I was standing here in this space with a feeling of accomplishment and happiness and satisfaction.

09:42:41 That is not the case.

09:42:43

09:42:44

09:42:45 But I am standing here.

09:42:48

09:42:49

09:42:50 I honestly can't imagine a world where that will ever be enough.

09:42:56

09:42:57 But it is something.

09:42:59 [Inaudible]

An Open Letter to All My Relations

Some of you I know.

Some of you I don't know.

This is not my fault. This is not your fault.

But it is a fact.

I wish I knew all of you. I wish I had grown up knowing all of you.

The truth, though, is that many of you are complete strangers.

I don't know what to do with that.

Except to say that there were certain circumstances that made it this way.

Those circumstances are the subject of this book.

I have struggled greatly with how to tell this story.

Because it is not just my story but all of our stories intertwined.

For example, it is not possible to tell just my story of intergenerational trauma.

Because it involves both the generations before and after mine.

And this is a book for all of those generations.

This is a book for me.

This is a book for you.

This is a book for everyone.

I held off writing this book for such a long time.

To tell you the truth, I often wish I had never decided to start writing this book.

Many of the details and stories and realizations and admissions are painful for me.

Throughout the process of writing this book I have experienced intense feelings of loneliness, isolation, depression, anxiety, and thoughts of suicide.

I haven't really told anyone about these feelings.

But they are real and they are wrapped up somewhere in all of these feelings about being an intergenerational survivor of Residential School, of being an urban Indigenous person, and of being "doubly dispossessed" (from both Nisga'a land and knowledge), as my friend Natalie Knight eloquently put it.

I'm writing this book and stating these things as honestly as I can because it has become necessary for me to stop holding it inside.

I'm writing this open letter to you because this book is about us.

I'm hoping that when you read this, you will find something helpful, something of value.

I know these things are hard to talk about.

That's actually one of the reasons that I have continued to write this book.

Because every now and then, someone will come up to me after I've talked about this project and tell me that something very similar has happened in their family.

That they haven't been able to put it into words until now.

To be honest, I wish this book had been written years ago by someone else.

But here we are.

I'm writing you this letter to tell you that you're not alone.

We may not all experience it in the same way, but many of us are in similar positions.

I've felt so alone in my life when it comes to this kind of stuff.

So these words are probably just as much for me as they are for you.

But I think this is an important thing to say.

And I think it helps to talk openly and honestly about our experiences because so many people (both Indigenous and non-Indigenous) don't recognize the kinds of privilege that come with having access to Indigenous knowledge and culture.

So many don't understand what experiences of intergenerational trauma actually look like.

So many don't really get why so many Indigenous youth are committing suicide.

So many don't understand our actual experiences of Indigeneity.

So many don't care to think about how deeply we are impacted by colonialism and attempted genocide.

I also wanted to say that you don't have to be anything more or less than who you are right now.

I feel as though there is all kinds of pressure from both Indigenous and non-Indigenous Peoples to be Indigenous in a certain way.

I have to admit that I still feel this pressure, but I'm doing my best to be Indigenous in my own way.

I think I am healthier being okay with who I am.

And if this is helpful for you in any way, I think you're better off being okay with who you are, too.

I wish we were closer.

I wish we could get everyone together. In the same room. All of the brothers and sisters and aunties and uncles and cousins and grandparents.

I wish we could all talk to each other.

Maybe someday that will happen.

But in the meantime, I want you to know that I'm thinking about all of you.

I'm thinking about all of you that I know.

I'm thinking about all of you that I don't know.

Acknowledgements

This book would not have been possible without my parents—Catherine Abel and Lawrence Wilson—while this has been an incredibly difficult journey for all of us, I want you to know that you are both always in my thoughts even if the path to repairing our relationships seems, at times, an impossibility.

This book would also not have been possible without my Aunt Bonnie who was always willing to talk to me even though our talks were very often about the most difficult things. Thank you for your time, your generosity, and your understanding.

I am so deeply grateful and humbled by everyone that was willing to read early versions of this book. Especially to my partner, Chelsea Novak, who always has the keenest eye and always asks the toughest questions with grace and care. Chelsea, you have always been the very best first reader of my work and first listener to all of my ideas. I can't thank you enough. Especially for listening to all my ideas over the years that have gone absolutely nowhere. And my sincerest thank you to Josh Whitehead, Billy-Ray Belcourt, Tenille Campbell, Alicia Elliott, Maddie Reddon, Richard Van Camp, and Gregory Scofield for your incredible generosity and your kind words of support.

I would also like to thank my absolutely wonderful Ph.D. committee at Simon Fraser University—Sophie McCall, Stephen Collis, Deanna Reder, David Chariandy, June Scudeler, Warren Cariou, and Clint Burnham—for all of the countless hours that you spent with me, for all your generosity, and for all the times you fought to make space for this kind of writing. This book would not have happened without your deep thoughtfulness and care. Likewise, I would also like to thank Jeff Derksen and Matt Hussey for not only championing this work, but also making the time and space for it.

My deepest thanks, too, to everyone at the University of Alberta's English and Film Studies department—especially to Keavy Martin, Marilyn Dumont, Mike Litwak, Julie Rak, Danielle Fuller, Christine Stewart, Peter Sinnema, and Mike O'Driscoll—for welcoming me and my work into a new home. I am so honoured and grateful to be here, and I so appreciate the time and space you gave to me to finish off this project.

Much of this work, as you've seen in the book, was presented at—and written for—conference and symposium presentations over the last few years, and I am so thankful to all of the organizers of the Mikinaakominis / Transcandas: Literature, Justice, Relation conference, SFU's Print Culture Speakers Series, the University of Victoria's Digital Humanities Summer Institute, the Symposium for Indigenous New Media, the Critical Nationalisms & Counter-Publics symposium, and Selkirk College's Reconciliation Speakers Series for inviting me to present my work; and especially to Smaro Kamboureli, Larissa Lai, Maddie Reddon, Leah Lychowyd, Matt Hussey, Dave Gaertner, Ray Siemens, and Alyssa Arbuckle for the invitations and the organizing. Parts of this work were also presented at—and written for—job talks that I presented at the University of Windsor, the University of Saskatchewan, Simon Fraser University, and the University of Alberta, and I am so deeply grateful to everyone that brought me out and asked me questions, especially Sophie McCall, Deanna Reder, Stephen Collis, David Chariandy, Joanne Leow, Susan Holbrook, Louis Cabri, Nicole Markotic, Keavy Martin, and Marilyn Dumont.

I would also like to thank Warren Cariou, Alison Calder, and the University of Manitoba's Centre for Creative Writing and Oral Culture for inviting me to work on this book during my residency in Winnipeg, and for your wonderful hospitality. I am especially grateful to Warren Cariou for also being an editor for this book—your brilliant editorial eye lifted up the very best of this work.

While this book has many points of origin, one of them was Sachiko Murakami's interview with me on her website *The Hardest Thing About Being a Writer*. Thank you so much, Sachiko, for the discussion and for your brilliant questions and insights. This interview was one of the very first moments when I started to talk openly and honestly about my experiences as both an intergenerational survivor of Residential Schools but also about my experiences within the Canadian literary scene. Likewise, I'd very much like to thank Cecily Nicholson for thinking through this work so carefully and for our amazing dialogue in *Rungh* magazine.

And thank you to everyone who believed in this work early on and published early excerpts/pieces, including editors Jason Camlot and Katherine McLeod for *CanLit Across Media: Unarchiving the Literary Event*, and guest editors Sophie McCall and Deanna Reder for *ARIEL: A Review of International English Literature*.

My sincerest thanks to my agent Stephanie Sinclair for believing in me and my work.

And last but not least, my utmost gratitude to Jared Bland and everyone at McClelland & Stewart for all the time and effort you've put into this project, for believing in this work, and for making this book a reality. Thank you!

Hardcover edition published 2021

McClelland & Stewart and colophon are registered trademarks of
Penguin Random House Canada Limited.

Library and Archives Canada Cataloguing in Publication data is
available upon request.

ISBN: 978-0-7710-0790-3
ebook ISBN: 978-0-7710-0791-0

The interview from "The Hardest Thing About Being a Writer," originally published January 12, 2017, is used with the permission of Sachiko Murakami.

Cover art by Jordan Abel
Cover design by Terri Nimmo

Typeset in Sabon by M&S, Toronto
Printed in the United States of America

McClelland & Stewart,
a division of Penguin Random House Canada Limited,
a Penguin Random House Company
www.penguinrandomhouse.ca

3rd Printing